First World War
and Army of Occupation
War Diary
France, Belgium and Germany

48 DIVISION
Headquarters, Branches and Services
Royal Army Ordnance Corps
Deputy Assistant Director Ordnance Services
2 April 1915 - 31 October 1917

WO95/2748/3

The Naval & Military Press Ltd
www.nmarchive.com
Published in association with The National Archives

Published by

The Naval & Military Press Ltd

Unit 10 Ridgewood Industrial Park,

Uckfield, East Sussex,

TN22 5QE England

Tel: +44 (0) 1825 749494

www.naval-military-press.com

www.nmarchive.com

This diary has been reprinted in facsimile from the original. Any imperfections are inevitably reproduced and the quality may fall short of modern type and cartographic standards.

© **Crown Copyright**
Images reproduced by permission of The National Archives, London, England, 2015.

Contents

Document type	Place/Title	Date From	Date To
Heading	WO95/2748 48 Div Apr 15-Oct 17 Dep Asst Direct Ordnance Services		
Heading	48th Division D.A. Dir Ordnance Services Apr 1915 Oct 1917		
Heading	DADOS South Midland Division Vol I 2-28.4.15		
War Diary		02/04/1915	06/04/1915
War Diary	Merris	09/04/1915	16/04/1915
War Diary	Nieppe	17/04/1915	28/04/1915
Heading	DADOS 48th Division Vol II 5-31.5.15		
War Diary	Nieppe	05/05/1915	31/05/1915
Heading	48th Division DADOS 48th Division Vol III 5-29.6.15		
War Diary	Nieppe	05/06/1915	11/06/1915
Miscellaneous	Large Percentage of Windows of Smoke Helmets Show Become Mix		
War Diary	Nieppe	11/06/1915	27/06/1915
War Diary	Lillers	29/06/1915	29/06/1915
Heading	48th Division DADOS 48th Division Vol IV July 1915		
Heading	War Diary Of (D.A.D.O.S. 48th (S.M.D) Divn) (Major & Warwick A.O.D) From 1-7-15 To 31-7-15		
War Diary	Lillers	01/07/1915	16/07/1915
War Diary	Terramesnil	18/07/1915	18/07/1915
War Diary	Authie	21/07/1915	27/07/1915
Heading	48th Division DADOS 48th Division Vol V 1-31.8.15		
Heading	War Diary Of Major Warwick and D.A.D.O.S. 48th Division From 1-8-15 To 31-8-15		
War Diary	Authie	01/08/1915	01/08/1915
War Diary	Bus	06/08/1915	29/08/1915
Heading	48th Division DADOS 48th Division Vol VI Sept 15		
Heading	War Diary Of Major Warwick D.A.D.O.S. 48th Division From 1-9-15 To 30-9-15		
War Diary	Bus	02/09/1915	26/09/1915
Heading	D.A.D.O.S. 48th Division Vol VII Oct 15		
Heading	War Diary Of Major Warwick D.A.D.O.S. 48th Division From 1st To 31st October 1915		
War Diary	Bus	03/10/1915	26/10/1915
Heading	War Diary Of Major H.B. Warwick A.O.D D.A.D.O.S. 48th Div. From 1-11-15 To 30-11-15		
War Diary	Bus	03/11/1915	19/11/1915
Heading	War Diary Of D.A.D.O.S. 51st Division From 1-11-15-30-11-15 Vol VII		
War Diary	Senlis	01/11/1915	30/11/1915
Heading	War Diary Of D.A.D.O.S. 48th Division From 1.12.15 To 31.12.15 Vol IX		
War Diary	Bus	04/12/1915	27/12/1915
Heading	DADOS 48th Div Jan Vol X		
Heading	War Diary Of Lieut B.M. Thomson A.O. Dept From 1-1-16 To 31-1-16		
War Diary	Bus	04/01/1916	28/01/1916
Heading	DADOS 48 Div Feb Vol XI		

Heading	War Diary Of Lieut B.M Thomson D.A.D.O.S. 48th Division From 1-2-16 To 29-2-16		
War Diary	Bus	12/02/1916	25/02/1916
Heading	War Diary Of Capt B.M. Thornton D.A.D.O.S. 48th Division From 1-3-16 To 31-3-16 Vol XII		
War Diary	Bus	05/03/1916	26/03/1916
War Diary	Colin	27/03/1916	28/03/1916
Heading	War Diary Of Capt B.M. Thornton A.O. Dept D.A.D.O.S. 48th Division From 1.4.16 To 30.4.16 Vol XIII		
War Diary	Couin	02/04/1916	24/04/1916
Heading	War Diary Of Capt B.M. Thornton A.O.D. D.A.D.O.S. 48 Div From 1-5-16 To 31-5-16		
War Diary	Couin	03/05/1916	31/05/1916
Heading	War Diary Of Capt B.M. Thornton A.O.D. D.A.D.O.S. 48th Division From 1-6-16 To 30-6-16		
War Diary	Couin	05/06/1916	30/06/1916
Heading	War Diary Of Capt B.M. Thornton A.O.D. D.A.D.O.S. 48th Division From 1-7-16 To 31-7-16 Vol 16		
War Diary	Couin	16/07/1916	16/07/1916
War Diary	Bouzincourt	19/07/1916	28/07/1916
War Diary	Domqueur	28/07/1916	31/07/1916
Heading	War Diary Of Capt B.M. Thornton A.O.D D.A.D.O.S. 48th Division From 1-8-16 To 31-8-16 Vol 17		
War Diary	Domqueur	02/08/1916	09/08/1916
War Diary	Beauval	09/08/1916	12/08/1916
War Diary	Bouzincourt	12/08/1916	28/08/1916
War Diary	Bus	29/08/1916	31/08/1916
Heading	War Diary Of Capt B.M. Thornton A.O.D D.A.D.O.S. 48th Division From 1-9-16 To 30-9-16		
War Diary	Bus	02/09/1916	10/09/1916
War Diary	Beauval	16/09/1916	18/09/1916
War Diary	Bernaville	20/09/1916	30/09/1916
Heading	War Diary Of Capt B.M. Thornton A.O.D D.A.D.O.S. 48th Division From 1.10.16 To 31.10.16		
War Diary	Henu	01/10/1916	21/10/1916
War Diary	Doullens	23/10/1916	23/10/1916
War Diary	Bazieux	31/10/1916	31/10/1916
Heading	War Diary Of Capt B.M. Thornton A.O.D D.A.D.O.S. 48th Div From 1-11-16 To 30-11-16		
War Diary	Millencourt	02/11/1916	02/11/1916
War Diary	Becourt Hill	07/11/1916	26/11/1916
Heading	War Diary Of Capt B.M. Thornton A.O. Dept D.A.D.O.S. 48th Division From 1-12-16 To 31-12-16		
War Diary	Becourt Hill	27/11/1916	10/12/1916
War Diary	Albert	16/12/1916	31/12/1916
Heading	War Diary Capt B.M. Thornton A.O. Dept D.A.D.O.S. 48th Division From 1-1-17 To 31-1-17		
War Diary	Albert	01/01/1917	01/01/1917
War Diary	Bazieux	01/01/1917	10/01/1917
War Diary	Hallencourt	28/01/1917	28/01/1917
Heading	War Diary Of Capt B.M. Thornton A.O. Dept D.A.D.O.S. 48th Division From 1-2-17 To 28-2-17		
War Diary	Mericourt Fun Farms	03/02/1917	03/02/1917
War Diary	Cappy	03/02/1917	28/02/1917

Heading	War Diary Of Capt B.M. Thornton A.O.D D.A.D.O.S. 48th Division From 1-3-17 To 31-3-17		
War Diary	Cappy	02/03/1917	25/03/1917
War Diary	Peronne	27/03/1917	30/03/1917
Heading	War Diary Of Capt B.M. Thornton A.O.D D.A.D.O.S. 48th Division From 1-4-17 To 30-4-17		
War Diary	Peronne	02/04/1917	06/04/1917
War Diary	Tincourt	11/04/1917	26/04/1917
War Diary	K 11.c.1.0	27/04/1917	29/04/1917
Heading	War Diary Of Capt B.M. Thornton A.O.D D.A.D.O.S. 48 Division From 1.5.17 To 31.5.17		
War Diary	K.11.c.1.0	03/05/1917	03/05/1917
War Diary	Flamicourt	03/05/1917	15/05/1917
War Diary	H.30.a.2.4	16/05/1917	20/05/1917
Heading	War Diary Of Capt B.M. Thornton A.O.D D.A.D.O.S. 48 Division From 1-6-17 To 30-6-17		
War Diary	H.30.a.2.4	0/206/1917	27/06/1917
Heading	War Diary Of Capt B.M. Thornton A.O.D D.A.D.O.S. 48 Division From 1-7-17 To 31-7-17		
War Diary	H.30.a.2.4	01/07/1917	01/07/1917
War Diary	Adanfer	04/07/1917	22/07/1917
War Diary	Janster Biezen	25/07/1917	31/07/1917
Heading	War Diary Capt B.M. Thornton A.O. Dept D.A.D.O.S. 48 Division From 1-8-17 To 31-8-17		
War Diary	Sheet 28 A30 B.5.4	02/08/1917	10/08/1917
War Diary	A.30.b.5.4	10/08/1917	29/08/1917
War Diary	Janster Biezen	29/08/1917	31/08/1917
Heading	War Diary Of Capt B.M. Thornton A.O. Dept D.A.D.O.S. 48 Division From 1-9-17 To 30-9-17		
War Diary	Janster Biezen	01/09/1917	17/09/1917
War Diary	Zutkerque	23/09/1917	24/09/1917
War Diary	A27D 50 Sheet 28	28/09/1917	30/09/1917
Heading	War Diary Of Capt B.M. Thornton A.O.D D.A.D.O.S. 48 Division From 1-10-17 To 31-10-17		
War Diary	A.27.d.50 Sheet 28	05/10/1917	07/10/1917
War Diary	G.1.b.1.8	11/10/1917	13/10/1917
War Diary	Pernes	14/10/1917	17/10/1917
War Diary	La Targette	17/10/1917	31/10/1917

WO 95/2748 (3)
48 Div
Apr 15 - Oct '17
Dep Asst Direct
Ordnance Services

48TH DIVISION

BEF

D.A.DIR.ORDNANCE SERVICES

APR 1915 - ~~FEB 1919~~

Oct 1917

To ITALY

121/5161

D.A.D.O.S. South Midland Division

Vol I. 2 - 28.4.15.

Army Form C. 2118.

WAR DIARY
or
INTELLIGENCE SUMMARY.
(Erase heading not required.)

April. 1915.

Instructions regarding War Diaries and Intelligence Summaries are contained in F. S. Regs., Part II. and the Staff Manual respectively. Title pages will be prepared in manuscript.

Place	Date	Hour	Summary of Events and Information	Remarks and references to Appendices
	2		Received first batch of recruits. Arranged for who wishes to be consigned for re-enlisted to a further new supply enough when transfer to be made to units	
	6		Began enquires under reforms of Warrant officers.	
MERRIS	9		Left for MERRIS	
	16		First consignment of arms received from Base. Moved from MERRIS to NIEPPE	
NIEPPE	17		Opened small ordnance store at LA CRECHE, at withdrawn store order 208 from infantry brigades for employment in store.	
	20		Opened divisional ammunition dump for refills & repairs at LA CRECHE; commenced by withdrawing ammunition Sgt. Major & two gunners from each brigade.	
	21		Received 6 machine guns & issued from to the Warwick & South Midland Infantry Brigades.	
	22		Received instructions from A.O. & 2.M.G. to endeavour to arrange to start a workshop to fit civilian forges & workmen. Fourteen travelling kitchens received.	

1577 Wt. W10791/1773 500,000 1/15 D. D. & L. A.D.S.S,/Forms/C. 2118.

April.

WAR DIARY
or
INTELLIGENCE SUMMARY.

Army Form C. 2118.

Place	Date	Hour	Summary of Events and Information	Remarks and references to Appendices
NIEPPE	23		14 travelling kitchens received	
	24		13 — do —	
	26		1 — do —	

Montagu L
Maj. DADOS.
April 30. 1915.

D.A.D.O.S. 48th Division

Vol II   5. - 31.5.15

Army Form C. 2118.

WAR DIARY
or
INTELLIGENCE SUMMARY
(Erase heading not required.)

Place	Date	Hour	Summary of Events and Information	Remarks and references to Appendices
NIEPPE	May 5.		Received four machine guns Maxim .303 from VI Div.; they require overhaul & their is being done	
	6		Issued above machine guns to 6/Glos & Worc Inf. Bde. — one per battalion. Under instruction from G.S. Wired Door Lashing above pipe attachments for M.G.'s — demanded along with (36).	//
	7		Received 20 sprayers & chemicals to issue in connection with dissemination of gases.	
	8		Received 16 additional sprayers	
	9		Following stores received for manufacture of respirators — 50,000 metres tape, 6500 pro goggles, 15,000 metres muslin; 15 sprayers & chemicals. Delivery of 1 ton cotton waste advised.	
	10		Received 1 ton cotton waste which has been issued together with above.	
	11	9-5	3 Corps wire — "Take over 13 limbered G.S. wagons from 9/Mid Div." an allotment 6"Div" refused 9/Mid Div — afterwards this 116/OD." Wired Inf. Bde Headquarters to return the 26 sprayers to Mty at A96 Ln Breteuil. Received 14 additional sprayers	

WAR DIARY
or
INTELLIGENCE SUMMARY.
(Erase heading not required.)

Army Form C. 2118.

Place	Date	Hour	Summary of Events and Information	Remarks and references to Appendices
	12		Received two Cross firewires no 14. Surplus limbered G wagons (26) received from battalions, issued 13 to VI Divin. Orders received for withdrawal of Mark IV b GS – 25% at once, 25% on 17th & remainder on June 1st; issued necessary instructions to unit III Corps for two truckes on 14th & 16th.	
	13		Issued 11 limbered G.S wagons to batteries of this division as extra vehicles, also 1 to Warrant A.V.C or 1st Canadian Divin. Mechanization (S400) received from II Army, issued to 2 D of M.S.	
	14		First consignment of Mark IV returned to Paris.	
	15		Withdrawal of second lot of Mark IV b hastened to 24th.	
	16		Have received complaints from infantry battalions re machine guns & rifles, units do not appear to take advantage of the armourers attached to attention been drawn to this in div orders.	
	22		II Army letter 59/1 of 21/5/15 states that owing to increase in the number of units in the field Al DSS is unable to continue the system of telegraphing all rockets to the Base. Instructions issued to all units to submit rockets in duplicate of this both when spares from detail; a list of these were also sent with circular.	

1577 Wt. W10791/1773 500,000 1/15 D. D. & L.   A.D.S.S./Forms/C. 2118.

WAR DIARY
or
INTELLIGENCE SUMMARY.

Army Form C. 2118.

(Erase heading not required.)

Place	Date	Hour	Summary of Events and Information	Remarks and references to Appendices
	May 23		HQrs II Army Letter S.1/10 of 21 5/15 authorizes issue of 16 short rifles for men with rifle grenades to them units armed with long rifles — Twenty per brigade headquarters were issued, in substitution of earlier issue of short, or normal, a month ago.	
	26	3.30pm	II Army HC 2692 wires "It is impossible that all your men are in possession of respirators for protection against gases & that they are instructed in use of them & that they are always 'carried or worn'."	
	27	10.30am	II Army HC 2719 wires "A reserve of 7500 respirators has now to be held under divisional arrangements by each division. It not complete with this number of Hypo pattern demand should be put forward — Wire for numbers still required stating if they are to complete same." N.B.— There is a reserve of 3000 + 7000 of a different pattern now in course of conversion to approved pattern.	
		9pm	Ordnance III Corps telegraphs wires "one rifle with telescope allotted your division, can be obtained on demand." Received from Div 192 rum burden to be rifle when completely division to authorized scale, also 416 periscopes — 30 per batt— now issued.	

Army Form C. 2118.

WAR DIARY
or
INTELLIGENCE SUMMARY.
(Erase heading not required.)

Instructions regarding War Diaries and Intelligence Summaries are contained in F.S. Regs., Part II. and the Staff Manual respectively. Title pages will be prepared in manuscript.

Place	Date	Hour	Summary of Events and Information	Remarks and references to Appendices
NIEPPE	May 29		DADMS informs "no alf-a are to be taken to whom blanket wagons pending further instructions - 732 QX.	
	30		One rifle with telescopic sight received. Authorities 7500 received as chemical men; return of 7500 blankets made also offered.	
	31	11-15p	Schreve II Army AC 2657 wires "In reference to lanterns for blank returning T tubes for 15th B.L.C. It has reply blank returning T tubes not available our supply much reduced as immediate return will be made on receipt.	

[signature]
Maj. DADOS
6th (S. Mid.) Div.

1577 Wt. W10791/1773 500,000 1/15 D.D.&L.   A.D.S.S./Forms/C. 2118.

48th Division

121/5502

5039

Indian 48th Division

Vol III 5—27.6.15

Army Form C. 2118.

WAR DIARY
or
INTELLIGENCE SUMMARY.
(Erase heading not required.)

Instructions regarding War Diaries and Intelligence Summaries are contained in F. S. Regs., Part II. and the Staff Manual respectively. Title pages will be prepared in manuscript.

Place	Date	Hour	Summary of Events and Information	Remarks and references to Appendices
NIEPPE	June 5	5 pm	Ordnance Barn wires – No spare parts by complete spare part boxes available". This refers to battle of machine gun recently issued from M. Arm. Received about 3000 mg bottles, there are to be issued to infantry battalions, one per man for hypodermic. Authorities & bottles are to be carried in the water certainly available. A demand note on the subject has been published.	
	7		Carrier arms – BLC 15/m 180 & rifle carrier arms received & issued. Received watchment bags for replenishment of MG bottles, also 300 Vigilant fuses to be issued to 6 coys.	
	8			
	9		Issued circular letter to N.o.s. 143 Inf Brigade in full. A memo on use of replenishment sundries devoted by G.H.Q received; every item must be – known – of both a standard not to be resorted to. Further some of MP bottles as therefore cancelled, & replenishment of III Corps pattern will gradually be replaced by those of the official type. Beside the difficulty in being experienced in III army caps I.D. & pastilliers, the	
	11		but was revised at III Corps weekly conference. D.D.O.S. H.Q. letter of 9/4. anthropic a reserve of ammunition & one replenishment to army of the infantry, carrying Git., A.L & O.R.M.G. No details are given as to how these are to	

Large percentage
of windows of Smoke
Helmets soon become
ins:/

WAR DIARY
or
INTELLIGENCE SUMMARY.

Army Form C. 2118.

Place	Date	Hour	Summary of Events and Information	Remarks and references to Appendices
NIEPPE	June 11.		he carried it out & who knows to places; from a tank; but underlined that for 3.6 lorries would be necessary. Submitted thumb to D.a.a.n to supplies same.	
	14		143rd Inf Brigade completed with approved pattern entrenching & march helmets issued	
	15		to 144th Inf. Brigade	
			144th Inf Bde completed as regards entrenching	
			145th Inf Bde completed with march helmets & entrenching	
	19		All Art, R.E., div. troops & A.A.M.C. (except 1 Field Amb.) completed with helmets & entrenching	
	24		A large number of entrenching tool helmets are being exported as being unsuitable; arrangements carried out so far as possible but first, in the knowns they known they D.A.D.O.S. 46th Div made unsafe that they were exchanging 1 for the others	
LILLERS	27		Left NIEPPE & arrived BUSNES	
	29		Opened store & made return issues.	

W M Cumming
Maj. D.A.D.O.S
46 (S. Mid.) Div

48th Division

18/6/19

DADOS. 48th Division
Pt IV

Army Form C. 2118.

WAR DIARY
INTELLIGENCE SUMMARY.
(Erase heading not required.)

Instructions regarding War Diaries and Intelligence Summaries are contained in F.S. Regs., Part II. and the Staff Manual respectively. Title pages will be prepared in manuscript.

Hour, Date, Place	Summary of Events and Information	Remarks and references to Appendices
	Confidential. War Diary of:- (D.A.D.Of 48th (Smd.) Div.) (Major H Warwick A.O.D) From: 1-7-15. To. 31-7-15.	

WAR DIARY
INTELLIGENCE SUMMARY

Army Form C. 2118.

Place	Date	Hour	Summary of Events and Information	Remarks and references to Appendices
LILLERS	July 1		Opened store & office	
			DDOS I Army visited the store & office	
			16 units of the march from NIEPPE arrived. ashes of travelling kitchens Mk	
			limber – 2 boilers in NIEPPE or 12 Plns. have never come to light. The coils so strongly	
			not showing enough, it was deducted from 30/III III Corps that the matter shall be	
			referred till.	
	7		Received one MG cart for 7/I War in place of a gun out of action owing to breakdown plate	
	8		Received two MG carts for 5/9/I War for same reason as above	
	9		Received one MG from 1/Dev. for 5/I War completing them to establishment of 4 guns.	
	12		Received 48 Demand of wagons	
	16		Instructions received for disposal of remainder of blanket wagons – now are being returned by the train under the allotment	
			Information received that divisions to be re-armed with the 16 pr. two travelling kitchens "U" returned to Bases & two re-demanded to replace	

WAR DIARY or INTELLIGENCE SUMMARY

Army Form C. 2118.

Place	Date	Hour	Summary of Events and Information	Remarks and references to Appendices
	July 16	3 pm	Demand of wagons received returned to OO IV Corps tracks Ord. Commns wires "Demand 50 vermorel sprayers from Havre & send them when to send them added Ord 46 Div 2 rifles Ord Ncom Stores + Ord G & Q inform your Telephone armgs.	
TERRAMESNIL	19	1-15 am	Ord from Havre wires H + C Perform to send up 192 SAA + put them will on complete tools plus two batteries total 96 hrs. & send them on complete kit plus our battery + an amm col also 96 kits aan amm of most shells & w cartridge water 46 div reported not ammn.	Afflet- Terri'll 10 am.
AUTHIE	21		No stores received but send out lorries for which stores are held.	
	22		Spent 16 pr guns & wagons received; sent to amm-railhead & supply railhead. M.T. DD093/Army. Opened company depot on the AUTHIE–THIEVRES road.	
	25		Received 40 sprayers	
	26		Issued sprayers, catapults & a num of smoke helmets ammunition as hand stores 15 pr equipt. & wagon G.S. reported by EOA as turn of over destituted to destination	

Army Form C. 2118.

WAR DIARY
or
INTELLIGENCE SUMMARY.
(Erase heading not required.)

Instructions regarding War Diaries and Intelligence Summaries are contained in F. S. Regs., Part II. and the Staff Manual respectively. Title pages will be prepared in manuscript.

Place	Date	Hour	Summary of Events and Information	Remarks and references to Appendices
AUTHIE	1915 July 27		Copy of minute from ADMS "Ord. 3rd Army wires that owing to there from no all that your division are now liable to which they should be armed & cannot enlist to be put forward at once for guns & any additional bayonets required." MMc_____ Maj. DADOS 46th (9Mid) Divisn 27/7/15	

1577 Wt. W10791/1773 500,000 1/15 D. D. & L. A.D.S.S./Forms/C. 2118.

48th/Division

Box 2591

DADOS. 48th Division

Vol V

1 - 31. 5. 15

Army Form C. 2118.

WAR DIARY
or
INTELLIGENCE SUMMARY.
(*Erase heading not required.*)

Instructions regarding War Diaries and Intelligence Summaries are contained in F. S. Regs., Part II. and the Staff Manual respectively. Title pages will be prepared in manuscript.

Place	Date	Hour	Summary of Events and Information	Remarks and references to Appendices
			Confidential War Diary of Major Warwick A.O.D. D.A.D.O.S. 48th Division From 1-8-15 To 31-8-15 main march m march	

A.D.S.S./Forms/C. 2118.

WAR DIARY
INTELLIGENCE SUMMARY

Army Form C. 2118.

Place	Date	Hour	Summary of Events and Information	Remarks and references to Appendices
AUTHIE	Aug. 1		Received 7 machine guns & when issued as follows – 4 to 7/R War. Regt. & 3 to 7/R War. Regt. The guns released are being returned to store to serve to the Battalions of the Div. to complete them to establishment of four guns.	MWM
	6		Received visit from two officers of III Army; we explained some men of the 6/R War. who have been issued with a Lewis & were to prevent the waste of ammunition & machine habits; it was resolved in a wonderful saving in ammo.	MWM
	16		36 std Lewis received for trial; DDOS III Army came over. Received letter from III Army suggesting that units should make up all known rhs.	MWM
	26		Received 1120 Mills Rifle bombs; issue made to MG detachments & forward army. MG sec. Off. of infantry.	
	29		After visits to all Bdes in the area a review of spts from O.C. units estimate % old hands called & made up & 40% – 45% of men is trained. III Army drew attention to the excessive issue made to certain divisions. Received two Bn. Lewis guns for issue to 7/9/8/ Warwick Regt.	MWM

W.M. Mortimer
Md.g.D.O.S.
48th Div.

1469/121

48th Division

DADOS 48th Division
Vol XL
Sept. 15

Army Form C. 2118.

WAR DIARY
or
INTELLIGENCE SUMMARY.

(Erase heading not required.)

Confidential

War Diary
of
Major Warwick
A.D.M.S. 48th Division

From 1-9-15 To 30-9-15

Army Form C. 2118.

WAR DIARY
or
INTELLIGENCE SUMMARY.
(Erase heading not required.)

Instructions regarding War Diaries and Intelligence Summaries are contained in F. S. Regs., Part II. and the Staff Manual respectively. Title pages will be prepared in manuscript.

Place	Date	Hour	Summary of Events and Information	Remarks and references to Appendices
BUS	Sept 2		Received Vickers gun for 5/Lincoln in exchange for Maxim to be available as Maxim	
	5	5.30p	Ord. Marine wires "This morning one Vickers each 4/R.Ducks & 1/Duke" + +	
	6	11-15am	Ord III Army wires "Submit indent for Maxims to complete to scale of one per man"	
	15		Received 250 tube helmets.	}mm
	16		Received 6 Webb's bomb throwers, instructed to arm them from 1/6 143 Inf Bde a form to 1/5 145 Inf Bde, to be marked as hand stores. Also received 2030 tube helmets making a total of 7946 received; issues made to infantry 5376, Ord 1560, OB 60 leaving balance of 950 for issue to infantry.	
	17		Ord. III Army wires (ref Ord. D12ML) states "Verbs for rifles now available aaa which should be founded for 250 per division on proportion of 2/5 short which & 3/5 long into further supply of 1550 tube helmets received, also first consignment of rifles not english for H.V. amm. in exchange for those english for H.V. amm - made with OYB 1613	Demand J348g/17/9 }mm
	19		Following memorandum received from 145 Inf. Bde from this D12ML "Y5604 rifles not enfiladed as issued by 144 & 2ML today aaa From our my Y6506 & 19" a Y6545 & 21 are rifles enfiladed then 4/Oxford km 25 pairs of hedges aa"	}mm
	24		One 4/7 Winchester Rocks 36 5 for 46 Oxfords 46 aaa no definite news made good Indents here only been received from 4/Oxfords for 15 pairs from hedges & Winchester 4/Ducks	}mm

WAR DIARY
or
INTELLIGENCE SUMMARY.

Date	Hour	Summary of Events and Information	Remarks and references to Appendices
25		4g; the letter are apparently not required as their establishment is complete. Ord. III Army wires "following are available & can be drawn from Heavy Mobile Workshops aaa heavy lys no 42. 4 hys lys no 43 – 20." Drew show hys & issued them to Hd qrs Divnl artly.	MWW
26			

McMorrow L
Major DADOS (MT) Div
30/9/15

12/7384

D.A.D.O.S. 4th Division

Vol VIII

Oct 15

Army Form C. 2118

WAR DIARY
or
INTELLIGENCE SUMMARY.

(Erase heading not required.)

Confidential

War Diary

of

Major Warwick, D.A.D.O.S., 48th Division.

From 1st to 31st October, 1915.

Army Form C. 2118

WAR DIARY
or
INTELLIGENCE SUMMARY.
(Erase heading not required.)

Instructions regarding War Diaries and Intelligence Summaries are contained in F. S. Regs., Part II. and the Staff Manual respectively. Title pages will be prepared in manuscript.

Place	Date	Hour	Summary of Events and Information	Remarks and references to Appendices
BUS	1915			
	3/10		Received one gun maxim ·303 converted to replace unserviceable for 8/Worc.	} nom/
	6/10		Received AF G 1096-181 for a Div. d'Armée Col.	
	9/10	11·45am	Following were received from III Army thro 7th Corps "Following arms appeared in gun posts this 225 to each of 37th & 46th div. no fl. were in trenches only new plain carr. bolt what to be forwarded under authority OB 5003/1476 engs. ones to return." – Both without trigger. At 7th Corps wire ref. my Q359 advance III Army were being two plain & full arms who should be demanded for each pair of gun bolts which ends.	
	13/10	6·10pm	As a result of a complaint from 143 Inf. Bde. concerning short arm long rifles, which were returned to Armoury for special inspection, found bands were but not "V" jamb was complained of, but after cleaning it was found that there was little to choose between them & the short rifle against which they were tested. Generally speaking new duty, two ounces oil wool & minhpus over to oil under their follower. Ordered III Army wires "Instr. for cared oil blocks should not be forwarded to Div. Until full instructions."	nom/
	16/10			nom.

WAR DIARY
or
INTELLIGENCE SUMMARY.
(Erase heading not required.)

Army Form C. 2118

Place	Date	Hour	Summary of Events and Information	Remarks and references to Appendices
BUS	16/10	10.30am	Ack. 7th Corps wire "Two cases w/k containing unidentifiable handloom to your representation at midnight this evening."	hm
	20/10		Received 15 Mobile Very Pistols.	
		7.20pm	7th Corps wires "Wire chief to DDOS III Army number of unmixed rifles you have in store with indent & wire must be sent tonight - repeated to this office as chief rifles only required."	hm
	26/10	6.15pm	Ack. 3rd Army wire Z649 "asc adaptors for tubes friction 2s about are to be drawn from H.M. workshops & issued to 66th & 100th hand mortar Btys & 100th trench mortar Bty a tomorrow and copy of instructions will be issued with each adaptor."	hm

hmMunich
Maj. DADOS
66th Divn

Army Form C. 21

WAR DIARY
or
INTELLIGENCE SUMMARY.
(Erase heading not required.)

Confidential

War Diary
of

Major F.B. Warwick, A.D.
D.A.D.S., 48th Div:

From 1-11-15 To 30-11-15

Vol VIII

WAR DIARY
or
INTELLIGENCE SUMMARY.
(Erase heading not required.)

Army Form C. 2118.

Place	Date	Hour	Summary of Events and Information	Remarks and references to Appendices
BUS	1915 Nov 3		Received telephone message asking numbers of long & short rifles in store; replied 40 long & 28 short, latter without bayonets. from DDoy III Army	MM
		11-50pm	DDoy III Army wires "issue 28 short rifles to 27th Divn on application." DADOS 36th Divn removed 100 Lists & JL brought into this divn area now time finished.	MM
	6		Received one MG from Divn to replace one unservicable belonging to 5/Inniskillings returned to Divn.	MM
			One storeman arrived via "Office" Anzrs ROD undergoing field punishment. Inspected ablutions, harness cleaning, ammunition & equipment in charge of the field companies OC 37th Divn. 1 MG car & 1 maxim belonging to 4/5 Glos Rgt found "U"; wired to Divn to replace. Issued gun parts this "completely" to 2025 for this divn. Received 10,000 anti-gas goggles.	
	16			MM
	19	4-15 pm	Ord Mazin wires "Demand of 2nd Blanket not yet received as an am prepared to revise it no state total requirements." Demanded by wire 1h 200 pairs of gum boots thigh in pursuance of the two attached battalions of M 36 & Divn on the "K" handed in to 48th Divn for these were on expiration of all these — Wire 36th Divn DADOS Q72.	MM

M Maun. K Maj. DADOS 46 Divn

Army Form C. 2118

WAR DIARY
or
INTELLIGENCE SUMMARY.
(Erase heading not required.)

Front Sheet -

Confidential

War Diary

of

A.D.M.S. 51st Division

From 1-11-15 — 30-11-15

Vol VII

121/7636

G.50.5

Whitby Capt.
A.D.M.S.
51st Division

WAR DIARY
or
INTELLIGENCE SUMMARY.
(Erase heading not required.)

Army Form C. 2

Instructions regarding War Diaries and Intelligence Summaries are contained in F. S. Regs., Part II. and the Staff Manual respectively. Title pages will be prepared in manuscript.

Place	Date	Hour	Summary of Events and Information	Remarks and references to Appendices
Serlis	1/1/15		Visited railhead & distributed stores to troops. Received 164 Jonah Stretchers from Ord Base. These with 40 purchased locally complete 14 Infantry Battalions with it for Company. The Stretchers are carried by two bearers & provide for the wounded to sit on the stretcher with back of patient being against the back of the front bearer. They are of special design to permit of the easy evacuation of wounded from narrow trenches.	10h
Serlis	2/1/15		Visited railhead & distributed stores to troops.	10h
Serlis	3/1/15		Visited railhead & distributed stores to troops. Patrols eliminating 12 such were issued today to complete H.Q. Infantry Brigade to 10, authorised establishment.	10h
Serlis	4/1/15		Visited railhead & distributed stores to troops.	10h
Serlis	5/1/15		Visited railhead & distributed stores to troops. Purchased locally 16 paraffin wall lamps for advanced dressing stations, as candles do not give sufficient light.	10h
Serlis	6/1/15		Visited railhead & distributed stores to troops. Received initial supply of 100 steel helmets	10h
Serlis	7/1/15		Visited railhead & distributed stores to troops. authorised at the rate of 50 per Inf. Battalion	10h
Serlis	8/1/15		Visited Railhead & distributed stores to troops.	10h
Serlis	9/1/15		Visited Railhead & distributed stores to troops. Received 20 stores loyers in lot of 50 allowed	10h

WAR DIARY
or
INTELLIGENCE SUMMARY.
(Erase heading not required.)

Army Form C. 2118

Instructions regarding War Diaries and Intelligence Summaries are contained in F. S. Regs., Part II. and the Staff Manual respectively. Title pages will be prepared in manuscript.

Place	Date	Hour	Summary of Events and Information	Remarks and references to Appendices
Serlis	10/4/15		Visited Railhead. Distributed stores to troops.	WM.
Serlis	11/4/15		Visited Railhead & distributed stores to troops.	WM.
Serlis	12/4/15		Visited Railhead & distributed stores to troops. 400 pairs of sheepskin boots received for distribution to mounted units where have been make it desirable that those boots should be used.	WM.
Serlis	13/4/15		Visited Railhead. Distributed stores to troops	WM.
Serlis	14/4/15		Visited Railhead. Distributed stores to troops. Proceed on 7 days leave to England this day. Work will be supervised by S. Cadet S.B. Carola ADC during my temporary absence	WM.
Serlis	15/4/15		Visited Railhead & distributed stores to troops.	SB
Serlis	16/4/15		Visited Railhead & distributed stores to troops.	SB
Serlis	17/4/15		Visited Railhead & distributed stores to troops. 2 transporting mounting received to-day. Nos 1 to 4 to R.H.A. James & 1 to 6 the Bde. Rifles.	SB
Serlis	18/4/15		Visited Railhead. Stores did not arrive. Received letter re 2" & 1½" Trench Mortars. Mortars in possession of 97th & 92nd Trench Mortar Batteries being sent, when arrangements made, to Heavy Mobile Workshops for overhaul & rebushing where necessary. Purchased 2 wallet cloths under instructions from Q.S. O.C. QMG for sending units to Trenches by rail. Army to Bn scale 17 rounds.	SB

1577 Wt. W10791/1773 500,000 1/15 D. D. & L. A.D.S.S./Forms/C. 2118.

WAR DIARY
or
INTELLIGENCE SUMMARY.
(Erase heading not required.)

Army Form C. 2118

Instructions regarding War Diaries and Intelligence Summaries are contained in F. S. Regs., Part II. and the Staff Manual respectively. Title pages will be prepared in manuscript.

Place	Date	Hour	Summary of Events and Information	Remarks and references to Appendices
Senlis	19/1/15		Visited Railheads and distributed stores to troops. Gentlemen's stores arrived today. Received 200 t home spun boots. They to be used by troops in trenches. Received further supply of footwear Kilmarnock.	6.
Senlis	20/1/15		Visited railheads and distributed stores to troops.	A
Senlis	21/1/15		Visited railheads and distributed stores to troops. Received 100 cttd helmets - further supply. Issued to 152 Bde.	A
Senlis	22/1/15		Received 1 Lewis machine gun complete for instruction. Visited railheads and distributed stores to troops.	6
Senlis	23/1/15		Visited railheads and distributed stores to troops. Received new component of wires (woods) (blanket).	A
Senlis	24/1/15		Returned duty on rejoining from leave. Visited railhead & distributed stores to troops.	W/r
Senlis	25/1/15		Visited railhead & distributed stores to troops.	W/r
Senlis	26/1/15		Visited railhead & distributed stores to troops.	W/r
Senlis	27/1/15		Visited railhead & distributed stores to troops. Went to Base for 1 heavy gun to replace one beyond local repair. Also for 1 Vickers gun to replace one beyond local repair for 1/6 Liverpool Regt. Received a further supply of 1800 Boots Gum Thigh for use of troops in trenches.	W/r
Senlis	28/1/15		Visited railhead & distributed stores to troops. Received 6 cases of musical instruments for Band Cond.	W/r

1577 Wt.W10791/1773 500,000 1/15 D.D.&L. A.D.S.S./Forms/C. 2118.

Army Form C. 2118.

WAR DIARY
or
INTELLIGENCE SUMMARY.
(Erase heading not required.)

Instructions regarding War Diaries and Intelligence Summaries are contained in F. S. Regs., Part II. and the Staff Manual respectively. Title pages will be prepared in manuscript.

Place	Date	Hour	Summary of Events and Information	Remarks and references to Appendices
Sailly	29/11/15		Vehicle rolled & distributed stores to troops. Wired for machine guns to replace others beyond local repair as follows: 1/6 Liverpool Regt. 1 Vickers gun — 2/5 Lancashire Fusiliers 1 Maxim.	Wh.
Sailly	30/11/15		Vehicle rolled & distributed stores to troops.	Wh.

Whalley Capt
Ad Bgd
51st Divn.

30/11/15

Army Form C. 2118.

WAR DIARY
or
INTELLIGENCE SUMMARY.
(Erase heading not required.)

"Confidential."

War Diary
of
D.A.D.O.S. 48th Division

From 1.12.15 to 31.12.15.

Vol IX

WAR DIARY
INTELLIGENCE SUMMARY

Army Form C. 2118.

Place	Date	Hour	Summary of Events and Information	Remarks and references to Appendices
BUS	Dec 4		Lt Thornton AOD joined. 4 - 60 pr guns & equipment arrived for 114 Hy Bat'y A.G.A. in exchange for 4.7" Q.F. one limber 16 pr received in turn for 60 pr ; 7 GS wagons returned to OO Dan	MOW
	5		4 - 4.7 QF returned two more spare & separate pond of equipt on exchange (including one officer of battery & arranged for eng return of these stores ; 7 GS wagons who returned ; on return of 6pr limber, receipt handed in to Lt Thornton.	MOW
	13		1 limbered G.S. wagon complete turnout received from No 4 Coy 3rd Div'l Train & handed over to No 1 & 68 Train ; this is the first of the 8 complete turnout requested for in front of Markes gun cop ; two limbered G.S. wagons & two skell arts of harness with harness saddlery.	MOW
	14		Received two limbered G.S. wagons & 2 shall arts of skell harness ; Following d arrived by G. "following" & mnal arrived CANAPLES afternoon 16th a.m. 46th Div - fr 143 144 & 145 Bde m g coys each ; cart-water / cart with horses L.D 3 drivers conveying 2 aaa Wagons limbered G.G. 7 Hrns LD 14 drivers conveying 7 aaa fr train wagons G.G. 3 Hrns HD 6 drivers AGB 3 aaa + + +	MOW
	16		On leaving III Army ware by pim imbuts shall be submitted at once for half pattern ... to compt. the two of this pattern on each Offinn are ... with DDOS & MQ 317/17 DT 14/15 - 7th Cops Q 99 16 14/15.	MOW

WAR DIARY
INTELLIGENCE SUMMARY

Army Form C. 2118.

Place	Date	Hour	Summary of Events and Information	Remarks and references to Appendices
BUS	Dec 20		Inspected grenade ammunition of 4th Divin as refered to 7th Corps	mm.
	21		Inspected grenade ammunition of 7th Corps	
	22		Inspected grenade ammunition of 37 Divn	B m T
	27		Major Warwick left the Division to take up the appointment of A.D.O.S. VII Corps	
	27		Lieut-Col Thornton took over the duties of D.A.D.O.S. from Major Warwick	

Am Thornton
A.D.O.S
D.A.D.O.S, 48th Division

Army Form C. 2118

WAR DIARY
~~INTELLIGENCE SUMMARY~~
(Erase heading not required.)

Instructions regarding War Diaries and Intelligence Summaries are contained in F. S. Regs., Part II. and the Staff Manual respectively. Title Pages will be prepared in manuscript.

Confidential

War Diary
of
Lieut. P.M. Thornton, R.P.Dept.

From 1-5-16 to 31-5-16.

Place	Date	Hour	Summary of Events and Information	Remarks and references to Appendices

[Stamp: D.A.D.O.S. 48th DIVISION]

Army Form C. 2118.

WAR DIARY
or
INTELLIGENCE SUMMARY.
(Erase heading not required.)

Instructions regarding War Diaries and Intelligence Summaries are contained in F. S. Regs., Part II. and the Staff Manual respectively. Title pages will be prepared in manuscript.

Place	Date	Hour	Summary of Events and Information	Remarks and references to Appendices
BuS.	1916. Jan 4th		51 Lewis Guns were received from the base and distributed to Units.	B.m Thornton O/C.
"	" 6th		4.5" Howitzer Equipment arrived & was taken over by 4th South Midland Howitzer Brigade.	B.m Thornton O/C.
"	" 13th		5" Howitzer Equipment was taken over from 4th South Midland Brigade & returned to the Base.	B.m Thornton O/C.
"	" 14th		Extract from Divisional Routine Order no 221 d/14/1/16. "S/lieut. B.m Thornton Army Ordnance Deptl &c. D.A.D.O.S. 48th Division vice Major R B Warwick, dated 22/12/15."	B.m Thornton O/C.
"	" 20th		Four Vickers Guns were received from 4th Division in exchange for 4.303 handed them by the 143rd Brigade. Exchange of machine guns between 144 and 145th Brigade was carried out. Thus giving each of the three Brigades 16 machine guns of similar type viz 143 Brigade 16 Vickers Guns, 144 Brigade 16 .303 Maxim Guns & 145th Brigade 16 converted .303 Maxim Guns.	B.m Thornton O/C.
"	" 25th		1. Lewis Gun was lost in action & 1 to replace was demanded from the base.	B.m Thornton O/C.
"	" 27th		5000 Tube Pattern Smoke Helmets for Divisional Reserve were received from Base.	B.m Thornton O/C.
"	" 28th		1 Lewis Gun received from Base to replace one lost in action and 16 Vickers Guns to replace 16 .303 converted held by 145th Brigade.	B.m Thornton O/C.

B.m Thornton
D.A.D.O.S.
48th Division

Dando S. 48 Div
Jul
Vol XI

WAR DIARY
—OR—
INTELLIGENCE SUMMARY
(Erase heading not required.)

Army Form C. 2118

Confidential

War Diary

of

Lieut. B.M. Lawson, D.A.D.S., 48th Division

From 1-2-16 to 29-2-16

Army Form C. 2118.

WAR DIARY
or
INTELLIGENCE SUMMARY.

(Erase heading not required.)

Instructions regarding War Diaries and Intelligence Summaries are contained in F. S. Regs., Part II. and the Staff Manual respectively. Title pages will be prepared in manuscript.

Place	Date	Hour	Summary of Events and Information	Remarks and references to Appendices
B.H.S.	1916. Feb. 12th		One .303 Vickers Gun was smashed by shell fire and one to replace this was demanded from the Base.	B.m.J.
"	" 15th		One .303 Vickers Gun received from Base issued to replace above.	B.m.J.
"	" 19th		One Lewis Gun was lost in action and one to replace was demanded from the Base.	B.m.J.
"	" 21st		One Lewis Gun received from Base to replace above.	B.m.J.
"	" 22nd		Two 2" Trench Mortars Reg. Nos 28 & 29 were converted to take rifle mechanism & re-issued to 100th Trench Mortar Battery	B.m.J.
"	" 25th		Instructions received to demand P.H. Smoke Helmets to replace 1 P. pattern per Officer & man. Indent submitted to Base 26/2/16.	B.m.J.

B.m. Thornton Lt
D.A.D.O.S. 48th Division

Army Form C. 2118.

WAR DIARY
INTELLIGENCE SUMMARY
(Erase heading not required.)

Instructions regarding War Diaries and Intelligence Summaries are contained in F. S. Regs., Part II. and the Staff Manual respectively. Title Pages will be prepared in manuscript.

Confidential

War Diary
of

Capt: R.T. Thompson, D.A.D.O.S
48th Division

From 1-3-16 to 31-3-16.

Vol XII

Place	Date	Hour	Summary of Events and Information	Remarks and references to Appendices

Army Form C. 2118

WAR DIARY
or
INTELLIGENCE SUMMARY
(Erase heading not required.)

Instructions regarding War Diaries and Intelligence Summaries are contained in F.S. Regs, Part II. and the Staff Manual respectively. Title Pages will be prepared in manuscript.

Place	Date	Hour	Summary of Events and Information	Remarks and references to Appendices
Bus	March 5th		Instructions received to demand an additional 2 Lewis Guns per Battalion. Autty OE y 867/4/3/46	Bm.Y
"	6th		Inst consignment of "P.H." Tube Helmets received & issued.	Bm.Y
"	"			B.m.Y.
"	10th		2000 additional Gun Rods (light) were allotted to the Division & demanded from the Base.	Bm.Y.
"	14th		48th Division was transferred from 7th Corps 3rd Army to 10th Corps 4th Army.	B.m.Y.
"	10th		System commenced of 1 Machine Gun per day being sent to the Divisional Armoury for overhaul.	B.m.Y.
"	13th		Division completed to 1 "P.H." Tube Helmet per Officer & Man	B.m.Y.
"	13th		Twenty-five Lewis Guns were received from the Base to complete to 6 guns per Battalion.	B.m.Y.
"	19th		1 B.L 60 pound gun demanded from Base to replace one condemned for wear by C.G.O. m 4th Army	B.m.Y
"	20th		Instructions received to demand ho 7 Dial Sights.	B.m.Y
"	21st		Two Lewis Guns demanded from Base to replace two damaged by Shell fire	B.m.Y
"	"		336 Respirating Towers (1st Supply) were received.	B.m.Y
"	"		Instructions were received to demand Equipment for 3 new 18 Pdr Batteries	B.m.Y
"	24th		Two Lewis Guns were received & issued to replace two damaged by Shell fire	B.m.Y
"	26th		The Division left Bus & went to Cuim	B.m.Y
Cuim	27th		Opened Depot & Armoury at Cuim	B.m.Y
"	"		ho 7 Dial Sights were received & issued.	B.m.Y
"	28th		Instructions were received to demand 2nd P.H. Tube Helmet.	B.m.Y

Bm Thomas Capt
D.A.D.O.S.

1875 Wt. W593/826 1,000,000 4/15 J.B.C. & A. A.D.S.S./Forms/C. 2118.

Army Form C. 2118.

48

D.A.D.O.S. April 16. 43rd DIVISION

WAR DIARY
INTELLIGENCE SUMMARY
(Erase heading not required.)

Instructions regarding War Diaries and Intelligence Summaries are contained in F.S. Regs., Part II. and the Staff Manual respectively. Title Pages will be prepared in manuscript.

Place	Date	Hour	Summary of Events and Information	Remarks and references to Appendices
			Conference War Diary of Capt. B.M. Thornton, A.D. Dept D.A.D.O.S. 48th Division From 1.4.16 to 30.4.16. Vol XIII	

Army Form C. 2118

WAR DIARY
INTELLIGENCE SUMMARY
(Erase heading not required.)

Instructions regarding War Diaries and Intelligence Summaries are contained in F. S. Regs., Part II. and the Staff Manual respectively. Title Pages will be prepared in manuscript.

Place	Date	Hour	Summary of Events and Information	Remarks and references to Appendices
Cassel	April 2nd		1 Lewis Gun damaged by shell fire & one to replace was demanded from Base	B.m.T.
"	" 3rd		1 .303 Maxim was returned to the Armoury past local repair and one to replace was demanded from Base	B.m.T.
"	"		1 Lewis Gun damaged by shell fire & one to replace was demanded from Base	B.m.T.
"	"		2nd G.A. Tube Helmets were received from the Base & were issued to replace "P" Helmets	B.m.T.
"	" 5th		1 Lewis Gun received from Base to replace one damaged on 2nd inst.	B.m.T.
"	"		1 B.L. 60 Pdr Gun arrived from Base to replace one condemned as the latter was returned	B.m.T.
"	" 6th		1 .303 Maxim Gun received from Base to replace those damaged on April 3rd	B.m.T.
"	" 8th		Received instructions as to disposal of winter clothing	B.m.T.
"	" 14th		2 - 1½", 1 - 3.7" and 2 - 4" Trench Mortar Batteries were withdrawn & returned to the Base	B.m.T.
"	" 15th		1 Lewis Gun damaged from Base to replace one damaged by shell fire	B.m.T.
"	" 17th		1 Lewis Gun received from Base to replace above	B.m.T.
"	" 19th		20,000 P.H. Helmets were received from the Base for Divisional Reserve	B.m.T.
"	" 24th		26 Lewis Guns arrived from the Base completing the Division to 8 guns per Battalion	B.m.T.

B.m.Thornton Capt.
D.A.D.O.S. 48th Division

Army Form C. 2118

WAR DIARY
INTELLIGENCE SUMMARY
(Erase heading not required.)

Instructions regarding War Diaries and Intelligence Summaries are contained in F. S. Regs., Part II. and the Staff Manual respectively. Title Pages will be prepared in manuscript.

Place	Date	Hour	Summary of Events and Information	Remarks and references to Appendices
			Confidential. War Diary of Capt. B. McPherson, A.D. D.D.O.S., 48th Div. From 1-5-16 to 31-5-16	

Army Form C. 2118

WAR DIARY
or
INTELLIGENCE SUMMARY
(Erase heading not required.)

Place	Date	Hour	Summary of Events and Information	Remarks and references to Appendices
Cuim.	May 3rd		Received instructions re re-arming the Division with the Short-Rifle. Infrequent to equip all Infantry Battalions were demanded from Base.	A.m.S
	3rd		16 Vickers Guns were issued to 144 Brigade M.G. Coy in place of 16 Maxim Guns.	A.m.S
	4th		16 Maxim Guns were returned to the Base.	A.m.S
	5th		3 new 18 pdr Batteries arrived, completing the Division to 3 Brigades of 4 Batteries each in place of 3 Batteries.	A.m.S
	14th		The re-arming of the Division with the short-rifle commenced.	A.m.S
	15th		Instructions were received regarding the absorption of Brigade Ammunition Columns and the absorption of the Howitzer Batteries into the 18 pdr Brigades, to take effect from this date.	A.m.S
	22nd		One Lewis Gun was damaged by shell fire & one to replace demanded from Base	A.m.S
	26th		One Lewis Gun received from Base to replace above.	A.m.S
	31st		One 3" Stokes Gun was received from 4th Army to replace one damaged by a premature.	A.m.S

Om Thursd Capt-
D.A.D.O.S. 48th Division

Army Form C. 2118.
48

Vol 15

WAR DIARY
INTELLIGENCE SUMMARY
(Erase heading not required.)

Commenced
War Diary
of
Capt. R.M. Thomson R.N.
D.A.D.O.S. 48th Division

From 1-6-16 to 30-6-16.

WAR DIARY
or
INTELLIGENCE SUMMARY

(Erase heading not required.)

Army Form C. 2118

Instructions regarding War Diaries and Intelligence Summaries are contained in F. S. Regs., Part II. and the Staff Manual respectively. Title Pages will be prepared in manuscript.

Place	Date	Hour	Summary of Events and Information	Remarks and references to Appendices
Courn	5/8/16		One Lewis gun was damaged by shell fire & one to replace demanded from Base.	Bm T
"	7/6/16		Lewis Gun to replace above was received.	Bm T
"	15/6/16		Railhead moved from Candas to Belle Eglise	Bm T
"	21/6/16		9.45" French Mortar arrived from Base	Bm T
"	24/6/16		One 4.5 Howitzer damaged by a premature was condemned by I.O.M	Bm T
"	27/6/16		One 4.5 Howitzer to replace above was received from the Base	Bm T
"	28/6/16		Two 2" Trench Mortars were damaged & buried by shell fire and could not be reused. Two to replace were demanded from Base.	Bm T
"	29/6/16		Two 2" Trench Mortars to replace above were received from Base	Bm T
"	30/6/16		One Lewis gun damaged by shell fire & beyond local repair, one to replace was demanded from Base.	Bm T

B. M. Thornley Captain
D. A. D. O. S. 48th Division
30/6/16.

…

Vol 16

Conference
War Diary
of
Capt. B.M. Thurnam ADC
D.A.D.O.S. of 5th Division
From 1-7-16 to 31-7-16

WAR DIARY or INTELLIGENCE SUMMARY

Army Form C. 2118

(Erase heading not required.)

Instructions regarding War Diaries and Intelligence Summaries are contained in F. S. Regs., Part II. and the Staff Manual respectively. Title Pages will be prepared in manuscript.

Place	Date	Hour	Summary of Events and Information	Remarks and references to Appendices
Corin	July 16"		Division moved from Corin to Bouzincourt.	A.m.J
Bouzincourt	July 19"		Two Lewis guns S/ 4th-Gloucester Regt & 2 Lewis Guns S/ 7th Worcesters, also 1 Vickers Gun S/ 144 M.G. Coy were all destroyed by shell fire & others to replace were demanded from Base.	B.m.J
"	"		2 Lewis Guns belonging to 7th Warwickshire Regt were reported lost & others to replace demanded from Base	B.m.J
"	" 20"		1 Vickers gun belonging to 144 M.G. Coy was reported destroyed by shell fire & one to replace demanded from base.	A.m.J
"	"		6 dung loads of salvaged stores including 1200 rifles were brought in to the Ordnance dump.	B.m.J
"	" 21"		Guns to replace those destroyed on 19/7/16 were received from Base, also the Vickers Gun for 144 Brigade M.G. Coy.	B.m.J
"	" 24"		1 Vickers Gun belonging to 144 Brigade M.G. Coy was destroyed by shell fire & one to replace demanded.	B.m.J
"	" 25"		2 Lewis Guns S/ 4th B". Oxford & Bucks, 2 S/ 1st B". S/ Warwick Regt & 2 S/ 6th B". Gloucester Regt were destroyed by shell fire & 6 to replace were demanded from Base.	A.m.J
"	25"		1 Lewis gun was received from A/Q". Division & issued to 5th B". Warwick Regt.	B.m.J

1875 Wt. W593/826 1,000,000 4/15 J.B.C. & A. A.D.S.S./Forms/C. 2118.

Army Form C. 2118

WAR DIARY
or
INTELLIGENCE SUMMARY
(Erase heading not required.)

Instructions regarding War Diaries and Intelligence Summaries are contained in F. S. Regs., Part II. and the Staff Manual respectively. Title Pages will be prepared in manuscript.

Place	Date	Hour	Summary of Events and Information	Remarks and references to Appendices
Bouzincourt	July 26th		Two Lewis Guns demanded for 4th Oxford & Bucks Bn & 1 for 8th Bn R. Warwickshire Regt were received from Base & issued to Units.	App J
"	" 27th		1 Vickers Gun for 144th Brigade M.G. Coy & 2 Lewis Guns for 6th Bn Gloucester Regt were received from the Base and issued to Units.	App J
"	" 28th		The Division moved from Bouzincourt to Donguieus.	App J
Donguieus	" 29th		Pumps and Armourers Staff were offered & Vickers Guns called in from Units for overhaul.	App J
"	" "		2 Lewis Guns for 4th Bn R. Bucks Regt were demanded from Base to replace two destroyed by Shell fire.	App J
"	" 30th		2 3"/1.5" Mortars demanded from Base to replace two belonging to 145th T.M. Battery destroyed by shell fire	App J
"	" 31st		2 Lewis Guns for 4th Bn R. Bucks Regt were received from Base to replace those destroyed by Shell fire.	App J

B.M.Thorold Captain
O.A.D.O.S 48th Division
31/7/16.

Army Form C. 2118

WAR DIARY
INTELLIGENCE SUMMARY
(Erase heading not required.)

Vol 17

Confidential
War Diary
of
Capt. B.M. Howard, A.D.
D.A.D.O.S. 48th Division
From 1-8-16 to 31-8-16

Army Form C. 2118

WAR DIARY
or
INTELLIGENCE SUMMARY
(Erase heading not required.)

Instructions regarding War Diaries and Intelligence Summaries are contained in F.S. Regs., Part II. and the Staff Manual respectively. Title Pages will be prepared in manuscript.

Place	Date	Hour	Summary of Events and Information	Remarks and references to Appendices
Domqueur	Aug 2nd		1 Vickers Gun was demanded for 1/4th Regt. M.G. Coy to replace one destroyed by shell fire and 1 Lewis Gun for 6th Bn. Glos. Regt to replace one lost in action.	R.m.Y
	" 3rd		1 Lewis Gun was demanded for 8th Bn. R. Warwick Regt to replace one lost in action	R.m.Y
	" 4th		1 Lewis Gun was demanded for 1st Ox & Bucks to replace one damaged by shell fire.	R.m.Y
	"		2. 3" Stokes were demanded received for 1/4 Sth Bn Battery to replace 2 destroyed by shell fire	R.m.Y
	3rd		1 Vickers Gun and 1 Lewis Gun demanded on Aug 2nd were received from the Base.	R.m.Y
	4th		1 Lewis Gun demanded on Aug 3rd was received from the Base.	R.m.Y
	5th		1 Lewis Gun demanded on Aug 4th was received from the Base.	R.m.Y
	7th		1 Carriage Field Q.F. 18 pdr complete was demanded for C 241 Brigade reported by G.O.C. on repair too long to carry out in the field.	R.m.Y
	"		The inspection of all Vickers Guns in the Division was completed.	R.m.Y
	8th		The Division moved to Beauval.	R.m.Y
Beauval	"		10 18 pdr guns & carriages complete were demanded for B 242. 3. C 242. 3. A 243. 2. B 243. 2., G.O.h having reported upon too long to carry out in the field.	R.m.Y

WAR DIARY
or
INTELLIGENCE SUMMARY
(Erase heading not required.)

Army Form C. 2118

Place	Date	Hour	Summary of Events and Information	Remarks and references to Appendices
Beauval	Aug 13th		The Division moved to Bouzincourt	R & T
Bouzincourt	"		The 10 Guns demanded on 9-8-16 were received from the Base.	R & T
"	" 15th		1 Carriage Field 18 pdr complete was demanded for B/241 Brigade. repairs too big to carry out in the field.	R & T
"	" 16th		1 Carriage field 18 pdr complete was demanded for C/241 Brigade. repairs too big to carry out in the field	R & T
"	"		2-3" Stokes were demanded for 1/45 Tm. Bty to replace 2 burned by shell fire.	R & T
"	"		1 Lewis gun for 5/15 Sherks & 2 for Bucks B[n] was demanded to replace one lost in action.	R & T
"	17th		The Carriage Field 18 pdr demanded on 15th inst. was received.	R & T
"	18th		The Carriage demanded Field 18 pdr demanded on 16th inst. was received	R & T
"	"		2- 3" Stokes Guns demanded on 15th inst. were received.	R & T
"	"		3 Lewis Guns demanded on 16th inst were received	R & T
"	20th		1 Carriage Field 18 pdr complete was demanded for C/241 Brigade, repairs too big to carry out in the field	R & T
"	"		1 Lewis Gun for 4th Ox & Bucks B[n] was demanded to replace one destroyed by Shell fire.	R & D.

Army Form C. 2118

WAR DIARY
or
INTELLIGENCE SUMMARY
(Erase heading not required.)

Instructions regarding War Diaries and Intelligence Summaries are contained in F.S. Regs., Part II. and the Staff Manual respectively. Title Pages will be prepared in manuscript.

Place	Date	Hour	Summary of Events and Information	Remarks and references to Appendices
Bougicourt	Aug 21st		1 Lewis Gun for 8th Bn. R. Warwick Regt was demanded to replace one destroyed by shell fire.	R.m.T
"	" 22nd		1. Carriage field 18 pdr demanded on 20th inst was received.	R.m.T
"	"		1 Lewis Gun demanded on 20th inst was received. also one demanded on 21.3" inst.	R.m.T
"	"		2 Lewis Guns were demanded for 5th Bn. R. Warwick Regt to replace 2 destroyed by shell fire	R.m.T
"	"		2 Lewis Guns were demanded for 6th Bn. R. Warwick Regt to replace one destroyed by shell fire and one lost in action	R.m.T
"	" 23rd		Two Lewis Guns for 5th Bn. Warwick Regt were received, also the two demanded for the 6th Bn. Warwick Regt.	R.m.T
"	"		1 Vickers Gun for 144th Brigade M.G. Coy was demanded to replace one destroyed by shell fire.	R.m.T
"	"		1 Q.F. 18 pdr without B.M. was demanded for C 241 Brigade to replace one teared	R.m.T
"	" 26th		1 Vickers Gun for 144th Brigade M.G. Coy was received	R.m.T
"	"		1 Q.F. 18 pdr for C 241. Brigade was received	R.m.T
"	"		The Division moved to Behencourt and Dolvain Sthn was opened at Bus.	R.m.T
Bus.	" 29		1 Lewis Gun was demanded for Bucks Bn. to replace one lost in action.	R.m.T
"	" 31		1 Lewis Gun for Bucks Bn. was received	R.m.T

1875 Wt. W593/826 1,000,000 4/15 J.B.C. & A. A.D.S.S./Forms/C. 2118.

WAR DIARY
or
INTELLIGENCE SUMMARY

Army Form C. 2118

Place	Date	Hour	Summary of Events and Information	Remarks and references to Appendices
Bus	Aug 31st		3 Lewis Guns were demanded for 8th Bn Warwick Regt to replace 3 lost in action and 2 Lewis Guns for 5th Bn Gloster Regt to replace two destroyed by Shell fire.	B m L

8th Division
31-8-16.

B. m Stewart Captain
D.A.D.O.S.

Army Form C. 2118.

WAR DIARY
~~INTELLIGENCE SUMMARY~~
(Erase heading not required.)

Vol 18

Confidential.

War Diary

of

Capt. B.M.T. London 2nd.
D.A.D.O.S. 48th Division.

From 1-9-16 to 30.9.16.

Army Form C. 2118.

WAR DIARY
or
INTELLIGENCE SUMMARY
(Erase heading not required.)

Place	Date	Hour	Summary of Events and Information	Remarks and references to Appendices
B.S.	1916 Sept 2nd		3 Lewis Guns were demanded for 5th R. Warwick Regt & 2 for 5th R. Ft Gloster Regt were received from the Base & issued	App V
	" 1st		1-18 pdr B.F. Gun & 1-18 pdr B.F. Gun Carriage were demanded for A 240 Bgde to replace others damaged by shell fire	App V
	" 3rd		The above Gun & Carriage were received from Base & issued	App V
	" 5th		24 - 3" Stokes mortars fitted with double Adaptors were received for issue in exchange for Mark I pattern.	App V
	" "		1-18 pdr B.F. Gun without breech fittings were demanded for B 241 Bgde to replace one condemned by A.O. in for repair.	App V
	" "		2-18 pdr B.F. Guns & Carriages were demanded for C 240 Bgde to replace others damaged by shell fire	App V
	" 7th		2-18 pdr Guns & Carriages for C 240 Bgde were received & issued	App V
	" 8th		1-18 pdr Gun for B 241 Bgde were received & issued.	App V
	" 10th		The Ordnance Stores were moved to Beauval.	

Army Form C. 2118.

WAR DIARY
or
INTELLIGENCE SUMMARY
(Erase heading not required.)

Instructions regarding War Diaries and Intelligence Summaries are contained in F.S. Regs., Part II. and the Staff Manual respectively. Title Pages will be prepared in manuscript.

Place	Date	Hour	Summary of Events and Information	Remarks and references to Appendices
Beaumel	Sept 16th		1- Vickers Gun for 14th Bgde M.G. Coy were exchanged to replace one beyond local repair	B.m.V.
	18th		The Division moved to Bernaville.	B.m.V.
Bernaville	20th		1- Vickers Gun for 14th Bgde M.G. Coy was received & issued	B.m.V
	24th		1- 17cm German howitzer was claimed by the Division as a trophy & was retained	B.m.V
			The Division was completed to 12 Lewis Gun Carts per Battalion.	B.m.V
	27th		1- G.S. 15pdr with B.m. hoodbound by G.O. for bilged bore and 1 carriage G.S. 15pdr completed to replace one "spares today & easy out in the field" were handed to from Base for C 240 Bde.	B.m.V
	30th		The Gun & Carriage demanded on 27th inst was received from the Base	B.m.V
			2 4.3" Stokes Guns fitted with tools adopter were withdrawn from the Division & replaced by the Mark I Pattern on transfer of the Division from the Reserve Army to III.rd Army	B.m.V
			The Division moved to Heinu on transfer to the III.rd Army	B.m.V

B.m.Yeu. Lt. Col
O.C. B.u.C. 48th Division

WAR DIARY
of
INTELLIGENCE SUMMARY

Vol 19

Conference
War Diary
of
Capt. B.M. Thornton. R.O.D.
D.A.D.O.S. 48th Division

From 1-10-16 To 31-10-16

Army Form C. 2118.

WAR DIARY
or
INTELLIGENCE SUMMARY
(Erase heading not required.)

Instructions regarding War Diaries and Intelligence Summaries are contained in F. S. Regs., Part II. and the Staff Manual respectively. Title Pages will be prepared in manuscript.

Place	Date	Hour	Summary of Events and Information	Remarks and references to Appendices
Henu	Oct 2nd		All 3" Stokes Guns fitted with Todd's Adapters were withdrawn from the Division and replaced by the 3" Stokes Gun Mark I	B→V
"	" 3rd		160m Blanks 13 were received from the Base & issued to units.	B→V
"	" 4th		2. 4.5" Howitzers without Bn's were demanded for D 241 Brigade to replace two condemned	B→V
"	" 5th		6, 9.0m for Cordite breech springs. Assistant Inspector of Armaments hitherto have demand for Temporary duty.	B→V
"	" 6th		2. 4.5" Howitzers without B.M. for D 240 Brigade & 1 for D 242 Brigade were demanded from Base & also 3 condemned by S.O.O for each breech springs	B→V
"	"		2 Vickers Guns were demanded for 143 Brigade in G. Coy to replace two beyond local repair.	B→V
"	" 7th		3. 4.5" Howitzers demanded on 6/10/16 were received from the Base.	B→V
"	" 8th		2. 4.5" Howitzers demanded on 4/10/16 were received from the Base	B→V
"	" 10th		2. 303 Vickers Guns demanded on 6/10/16 were received from the Base & issued to	B→V
"	" 15th		Assistant Inspector of Armourers hitherto Junior lent to the Division	B→V

Army Form C. 2118.

WAR DIARY
or
INTELLIGENCE SUMMARY

(Erase heading not required.)

Instructions regarding War Diaries and Intelligence Summaries are contained in F. S. Regs., Part II. and the Staff Manual respectively. Title Pages will be prepared in manuscript.

Place	Date	Hour	Summary of Events and Information	Remarks and references to Appendices
Hénin	28/10/16		The Division moved from Hénin to Boullens.	A.m.1
Boullens	29th		The Division moved to Bazieux.	B.m.1
Bazieux	31st		The Division moved from Bazieux to Millencourt Camp.	B.m.1
			116th Bde 31/10/16	
			B.m. Thornton Capt. D.A.D.O.S.	

Army Form C. 2118.

WAR DIARY
INTELLIGENCE SUMMARY
(Erase heading not required.)

Vol 20

Confidential
War Diary
of
Capt. B.M. Thornton ADC
Duport. 48/Div.
From 1-11-16 to 30-11-16.

Army Form C. 2118.

WAR DIARY
or
INTELLIGENCE SUMMARY
(Erase heading not required.)

Instructions regarding War Diaries and Intelligence Summaries are contained in F. S. Regs., Part II. and the Staff Manual respectively. Title Pages will be prepared in manuscript.

Place	Date	Hour	Summary of Events and Information	Remarks and references to Appendices
Millencourt	Nov 2nd		The Division moved from Millencourt to Bécourt Wood	Bm Y
Bécourt Wood	" 7th		One Lewis Gun was demanded for 6th Gloster to replace one destroyed by Shell fire.	Bm Y
	" 9th		The above gun was received & issued.	Bm Y
	" 12th		One Lewis Gun was demanded for Bucks Bn to replace one destroyed by Shell fire	Bm Y
	" 14th		The above Gun was received & issued.	Bm Y
	" 15th		1 Vickers Gun complete was demanded for 143 Brigade & 1 coy by plane one destroyed by Shell fire.	Bm Y
	" 17		The above gun was received & issued.	Bm Y
	" 18		The issue of winter clothing was completed	Bm Y
	" 19th		1 Lewis Gun was demanded for Bucks Bn to replace one destroyed by Shell fire	Bm Y
	" 20th		1 Lewis Gun was demanded for 4th Ox & Bucks Bn to replace one destroyed by Shell fire.	Bm Y
	" 25th		The Lewis Gun for Bucks Bn demanded on 23rd inst was received & issued.	Bm Y
	" 26th		The Lewis Gun for 4th Ox & Bucks Bn was received & issued.	Bm Y
	" 26th		The Division was completed to 2nd Blankets.	Bm Y

B. m. Monde Captain
D.A.D.O.S. 48th Division

Army Form C. 2118.

WAR DIARY
or
INTELLIGENCE SUMMARY
(Erase heading not required.)

Vol 21

Conference
War Diary
of
Capt. R.M. Thomson, A.D.Vet.
D.A.D.O.S, 5th Division
From 1-12-16 to 31-12-16

Army Form C. 2118.

WAR DIARY
or
INTELLIGENCE SUMMARY
(Erase heading not required.)

Instructions regarding War Diaries and Intelligence Summaries are contained in F. S. Regs., Part II. and the Staff Manual respectively. Title Pages will be prepared in manuscript.

Place	Date	Hour	Summary of Events and Information	Remarks and references to Appendices
Becourt-Hill	Nov 27th		D.A.D.O.S. was granted leave necessitating the inclusion of certain November entries in his December Diary.	BmY
" "	" "		2 .303 Vickers Guns complete were demanded for 143 M.G. Coy to replace others destroyed by shell fire.	BmY
" "	" 28th		1 - 18 pdr with B.M. & Carriage complete was demanded for C.241 Brigade to replace one totally destroyed by shell fire.	BmY
" "	" 28 "		1. 3" Stokes Gun was demanded for 144 I.M. Battery to replace one destroyed by shell fire.	BmY
" "	" 29 "		2 .303 Vickers Guns demanded on 27/11/16 were received from the Base and issued.	BmY
" "	" 30 "		1. 18 pdr Gun demanded on 28/11/16 was received from the Base and issued.	BmY
" "	Dec 5th		1. 303 Vickers gun was demanded for 143 M.G. Coy to replace one destroyed by shell fire.	BmY
" "	" "		12 Lewis Guns were demanded from Base to complete the Division to 2 per Bn	BmY
" "	" "		1. 3" Stokes gun demanded on 28/11/16 was received & issued	BmY
" "	" 4 "		12 Lewis Guns demanded on 1/12/16 was received from the Base and issued	BmY
" "	" 6 "		1. 303 Vickers Gun demanded on 5/12/16 was received from the Base and issued	BmY
" "	" 10 "		The Ordnance Dump was moved from Becourt-Hill to Albert	BmY

2449 Wt. W14957/M90 750,000 1/16 J.B.C. & A. Forms/C.2118/12.

Army Form C. 2118.

WAR DIARY
or
INTELLIGENCE SUMMARY
(Erase heading not required.)

Place	Date	Hour	Summary of Events and Information	Remarks and references to Appendices
Albert	Dec 18th		1 Lewis Gun was demanded for 4th R.F. Ox & Bucks L.I. to replace one destroyed by shell fire.	B m V
"	18/12		1 Lewis Gun demanded for 4th Ox & Bucks B.I. demanded on 18/12/16 was received from the Base & issued.	B m V
"	18/12		24 Lewis Guns to complete the Division to 12 per B.n were received from the Base & issued.	B m V
"	18/12		1 3" Stokes Gun was demanded for 143rd S.m. Battery to replace one destroyed by shell fire.	B m V
"	21/12		1 3" Stokes Gun demanded on 18/12/16 was received from the Base & issued.	B m V
"	22/12		1 4.5" Howitzer without B.m was demanded for C 242 Brigade to replace one condemned by G.O.m for wear.	B m V
"	23/12		The 4.5" Howitzer demanded on 22/12/16 was met by G.O.m with surplus gun in his possession.	B m V
"	30/12		1 18pdr gun without B.m was demanded for A 242 Brigade to replace one condemned by G.O.m for wearing.	B m V
"	31/12		1 Lewis Gun for heavy purposes was demanded from Base	B m V

B. m Purcell Captain
D.A.D.O.S. 48/Division

Army Form C. 2118.

WAR DIARY
INTELLIGENCE SUMMARY
(Erase heading not required.)

Instructions regarding War Diaries and Intelligence Summaries are contained in F. S. Regs., Part II. and the Staff Manual respectively. Title Pages will be prepared in manuscript.

Place	Date	Hour	Summary of Events and Information	Remarks and references to Appendices

Vol 2

Conference
War Diary
Capt. R.M.Johnson A.D.Pf.
Madts. to 8th Division
From 1-1-17 to 31-1-17

Army Form C. 2118.

WAR DIARY
or
INTELLIGENCE SUMMARY
(Erase heading not required.)

Instructions regarding War Diaries and Intelligence Summaries are contained in F. S. Regs., Part II. and the Staff Manual respectively. Title Pages will be prepared in manuscript.

Place	Date	Hour	Summary of Events and Information	Remarks and references to Appendices
Albert	1917 Jan 1st		The Division moved to Bayeaux.	B m T
Bayeux	" "		1-18 pdr gun without B.m. for A 242 Brigade was received from the Base and issued.	B m T
"	" 2nd		1. M.C. Vans without R.M. was demanded for D 241. Brigade to replace one condemned. 1 g 9.0.m. for excites envelopes in Breech end of Breechet.	B m T
"	" 3rd		1 - 303 Vickers gun was demanded for 143 Brigade M.G. Coy to replace one unserviceable.	B m T
"	" 4th		1. 18 pdr gun without B.m. was demanded for B 242 Brigade to replace one condemned by 9.0.m. for recoil.	B m T
"	" 5th		1 Lewis Gun issued for practice purpose was received from the Base & handed over to 3rd Corps School. 1 of 3rd Corps School.	B m T
"	" 6th		1. Vickers Gun demanded on 3rd inst. was received & issued.	B m T
"	" 8th		The Division moved to Hallencourt.	B m T
"	" 9th		1 - H.S. Howitzer without B.m. demanded on 1st inst. was received & issued through 50th Div.	B m T
"	" 10th		1 - 18 pdr gun without B.m. demanded on 4/1/17 was received & issued through 50th Divr.	B m T

Army Form C. 2118.

WAR DIARY
INTELLIGENCE SUMMARY
(Erase heading not required.)

Instructions regarding War Diaries and Intelligence Summaries are contained in F. S. Regs., Part II. and the Staff Manual respectively. Title Pages will be prepared in manuscript.

Place	Date	Hour	Summary of Events and Information	Remarks and references to Appendices
Hallencourt	Jan 28th		The Division moved to Maricourt-sur-Somme.	B.M. Rumbold Captain for A.A.G.S. 48/Division

2449 Wt. W14957/M90 750,000 1/16 J.B.C. & A. Forms/C.2118/12.

Army Form C. 2118.

WAR DIARY
or
INTELLIGENCE SUMMARY
(Erase heading not required.)

Instructions regarding War Diaries and Intelligence Summaries are contained in F. S. Regs., Part II. and the Staff Manual respectively. Title Pages will be prepared in manuscript.

Vol 23

Summary of Events and Information

Copy
of
War Diary
of
Capt. B. M. Stewart, R.A.M.C.
D.A.D.O.S. 48th Division
from 1-2-17 to 28-2-17

Place	Date	Hour		Remarks and references to Appendices

WAR DIARY
or
INTELLIGENCE SUMMARY

(Erase heading not required.)

Army Form C. 2118.

Instructions regarding War Diaries and Intelligence Summaries are contained in F. S. Regs., Part II. and the Staff Manual respectively. Title Pages will be prepared in manuscript.

Place	Date	Hour	Summary of Events and Information	Remarks and references to Appendices
Huiseard Sur Somme	1917 Feb 2nd		The Division moved to Cappy.	
Cappy	" 3rd		1. 4.5" Stores without Ammo was demanded for D/45 Brigade & replacement demanded by 9 am for week.	B m T
"	" 4th		Mr Humphrey joined the Division for instruction.	B m T
"	" 5th		24 Lewis Guns were demanded to complete the Division to M guns per Bn.	B m T
"	"		The first consignment of Small Box Respirators were received from the base for 143 m.G. Coy.	B m T
"	" 6th		3. .303 Vickers Guns were demanded from Base & replace 3 destroyed by Shell fire.	B m T
"	" 8th		2 Lewis guns were demanded for 6th Bn R. Warwickshire Regt to replace 2 destroyed by Shell fire.	B m T
"	" 9th		3. Vickers Guns demanded for 143 m.G. Coy.	B m T
"	"		1. 3" Stokes Mortar was demanded from Base to replace one burst for 243 T m Bty.	B m T
"	" 10th		1 Lewis Guns was demanded for 5th Bn R. Warwickshire Regt to replace one destroyed by Shell fire.	B m T
"	"		9 Lewis Guns demanded for 6th Bn R. Warwickshire Regt were received & issued.	B m T
"	" 12th		24 Lewis Guns were received from the base amplifying the Division to 14 per Bn.	B m T

WAR DIARY
or
INTELLIGENCE SUMMARY

Army Form C. 2118.

Place	Date	Hour	Summary of Events and Information	Remarks and references to Appendices
Cappy	Feb 12th		Lieut Humphry's A.O.D. left the Division	Anny
"	"		1- 3" Rifles demanded for 143 T.m. Battery was received issued	Anny
"	14th		1- 4.5" Stops without P.M. demanded on Feb 3rd for D240 Brigade was received	Anny
"	16th		1- Lewis Gun demanded on 11/2/17 for 5th R.F Warwickshire Regt was received & issued	B by
"	24th		1- .303 Vickers Gun was demanded for 143 M.G. by to replace one destroyed by Shell fire	B by
"	"		1- 2" T.m. was demanded for Z+S T.M. B.G. to replace one sent to Base by 3rd Army School	11 by
"	27th		1- .303 Vickers Gun demanded on 24/2/17 for 143 M.G. by was received & issued	12 by
"	"		1- 2" T.m. demanded on 24/2/17 for Z+S T.M. B.G. was received & issued	B by
"	"		1- Lewis Gun was demanded for 7th B= Worcester Regt to replace one destroyed by Shell fire	12 by
"	28th		1- Lewis Gun was demanded for 8th B= Worcester Regt to replace one destroyed by Shell fire	13 by

B.m. Thomas Captain
D.A.D.O.S. 48th Division

Army Form C. 2118.

WAR DIARY
INTELLIGENCE SUMMARY
(Erase heading not required.)

Vol 24

Copies of
War Diary
of
Capt. R.H. Thomson R.A.
D.A.D.O.S. 48th Division
From 1-3-17 to 31-3-17

Army Form C. 2118.

WAR DIARY
INTELLIGENCE SUMMARY
(Erase heading not required.)

Instructions regarding War Diaries and Intelligence Summaries are contained in F. S. Regs., Part II. and the Staff Manual respectively. Title Pages will be prepared in manuscript.

Place	Date	Hour	Summary of Events and Information	Remarks and references to Appendices
Cappy	March 2nd		1. Lewis Gun demanded for 7th Bn Worcester Regt was received & issued	18 m Y
"	" 4th		2. 3" Stokes were demanded for 145 T.m. Battery to replace 2 lost by 8th Corps School	18 m Y
"	"		1. Lewis Gun demanded for 8th Bn Worcester Regt was received & issued	18 m Y
"	"		2. 8" Stokes demanded for 145th T.m. Battery were received & issued	18 m Y
"	" 7th		1. Spdr gun carriage was demanded for T.B. 240 Brigade to replace one destroyed by Shellfire.	18 m Y
"	"		The Division was completed with Box Respirators & a reserve of 2000 completed.	18 m Y
"	" 8th		1. 18pdr gun with B.m. & with carriage was demanded for C 240 Brigade, the gun damaged by wear & the carriage by Shellfire.	18 m Y
"	" 10th		1. 15pdr gun carriage demanded for T.B. 240 Brigade was received & issued	18 m Y
"	" 12th		1. 18pdr gun & carriage demanded for C 240 Brigade was received & issued	18 m Y
"	" 15th		1. 303 Vickers Gun was demanded for 144 M.G. Coy to replace one destroyed by shellfire	18 m Y
"	" 18th		2. Barrels & 2 stands for 3" Stokes were demanded for 143 T.m. B.y to replace others	18 m Y
"	" 17th			
"	" 21st		1. 303 Vickers Gun demanded for 144 M.G. Coy was received & issued	18 m Y
"	" 22nd		3 Barrels & 2 stands for 3" Stokes demanded on 17/3/17 was received & issued	18 m Y

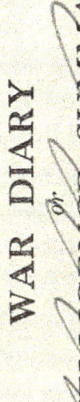

Army Form C. 2118.

WAR DIARY
or
INTELLIGENCE SUMMARY
(Erase heading not required.)

Instructions regarding War Diaries and Intelligence Summaries are contained in F.S. Regs., Part II. and the Staff Manual respectively. Title Pages will be prepared in manuscript.

Place	Date	Hour	Summary of Events and Information	Remarks and references to Appendices
Cappy	Mar 24th		1 Barrel for 2" T.m. was demanded for Y48 T.m Bty to replace one destroyed by premature	App. 7
"	" 25th		The Division moved to Peronne	App. 7
Peronne	" 27th		1 Barrel for 2" T.m demanded for Y48 T.m Battery was received & issued	App. 7
"	" 30th		2 - 18 pdr guns & carriages complete were demanded for B.241 Brigade to replace 2 condemned by 9.O.M for scoring & excessive wear	App. 8

Bm Townsend Captain
D.a.D.o.S. 48/Div I'am
31/3/17.

Army Form C. 2118.

WAR DIARY
or
INTELLIGENCE SUMMARY

(Erase heading not required.)

Vol 25

Correspondence
War Diary
of
Capt. B.M. London) R.D.
A.D.V.S. 47th Division
From 1-4-17 to 30-4-17

Army Form C. 2118.

WAR DIARY
or
INTELLIGENCE SUMMARY

(Erase heading not required.)

Instructions regarding War Diaries and Intelligence Summaries are contained in F. S. Regs., Part II. and the Staff Manual respectively. Title Pages will be prepared in manuscript.

Place	Date	Hour	Summary of Events and Information	Remarks and references to Appendices
Peronne	April 2nd 1919		24 Lewis guns to complete the Division to 16 per Battalion were received & issued.	B my T
"	" 6th		2 - 18 pdr guns & carriages complete were received for B 241 Brigade & issued.	B my T
"	" 6th		The Division moved to Sincourt	B my T
Sincourt	" 10th		1 - 18 pdr gun without B.m was demanded for A 241 Brigade to replace one condemned by G.O.m for Scoring.	B my T
"	" 14th		1 - 18 pdr gun with B.m was demanded for C 240 Brigade to replace one condemned for Scoring.	B my T
"	" 15th		1 Lewis Gun was demanded for 5/1st Glos Worcester Regt. to replace one destroyed by shell fire.	B my T
"	" 17th		2. 18 pdr guns demanded on 11th & wi 2 wite were received & issued.	B my T
"	"		1 - Lewis Gun demanded on 17th inst was received & issued	B my T
"	" 24th		The Division moved to K11 C10.	
"	" 25th		1 - 4.5" carriage was demanded for D 240 Brigade to replace one condemned by G.O.m.	B my T
"	" 26th		1 Lewis gun was demanded for 6th Bn Gloucester Regt. to replace one destroyed by Shell fire.	B my T

2449 Wt. W14957/M90 750,000 1/16 J.B.C. & A. Forms/C.2118/12.

Army Form C. 2118.

WAR DIARY
or
INTELLIGENCE SUMMARY
(Erase heading not required.)

Instructions regarding War Diaries and Intelligence Summaries are contained in F. S. Regs., Part II. and the Staff Manual respectively. Title Pages will be prepared in manuscript.

Place	Date	Hour	Summary of Events and Information	Remarks and references to Appendices
K1.C.1.0.	April 17		1. .303 Vickers Gun was demanded for 144 M.G. Coy to replace one destroyed by shell fire.	Appx.
"	"		2. Lewis Guns were demanded for 4th Bn. Gloucester Regt. to replace 2 destroyed by shell fire.	Appx.
"	"		3. Lewis Guns were demanded for 8th Bn. Worcester Regt. to replace 5 lost in action.	Appx.
"	29th		1. .303 Vickers Gun demanded on 27/4/17 for 144 M.G. Coy was received & issued.	Appx.
"	"		2. Lewis Guns for 4th Bn. Gloster Regt., Lewis Guns for 8th Bn. Gloster Regt. & 5 Lewis Guns for 8th Bn. Worcester Regt. demanded on 27/4/17 was received & issued	Appx.
	30/4/17			

B. M. Thornley Captain
D.A.D.O.S. 48/Division

Army Form C. 2118

Instructions regarding War Diaries and Intelligence Summaries are contained in F. S. Regs., Part II. and the Staff Manual respectively. Title Pages will be prepared in manuscript.

WAR DIARY
or
INTELLIGENCE SUMMARY
(Erase heading not required.)

Vol 26

Conference
War Diary
of
Capt. R.M.T Lorenzo, A.D
D.A.D.S. 48th Division
from 1.5.17 to 31.5.17

Place	Date	Hour	Summary of Events and Information	Remarks and references to Appendices

WAR DIARY
INTELLIGENCE SUMMARY
(Erase heading not required.)

Army Form C. 2118

Instructions regarding War Diaries and Intelligence Summaries are contained in F.S. Regs, Part II. and the Staff Manual respectively. Title Pages will be prepared in manuscript.

Place	Date	Hour	Summary of Events and Information	Remarks and references to Appendices
1917 Kii.C.1.0. Flaviecourt	May 3rd		The Division moved to Flavicourt. Personne.	B m y
	"		1. 18 pdr gun without B.m. was demanded for A.240 Brigade to replace one condemned by 9.0.h. for scoring.	B m y
"	" 4th		1. 18 pdr gun with B m was demanded for B. 241 Brigade to replace one condemned by 9.O.h. for scoring.	B m y
"	"		1. H.S. Howr. carriage demanded on 23/4/17 was received & issued.	B m y
"	" 8 15		1 - 18 pdr gun with B.M. was demanded for C.240 Brigade to replace one condemned by 9.O.h. for scoring.	B m y
"	" 10 -		2 - 18 pdr guns demanded on 4/5/17 for A.240 Brigade & B.241 Brigade were received from the B&S. & issued.	B m y
"	" 12 15		1 - 18 pdr carriage was demanded for C 241 Brigade to replace one condemned by 9.O.h.	B m y
"	" 13 15		The Division moved to Beaulencourt. Dump was formed on Bapaume - Fremicourt road.	B m y
H30.a.2.4.	" 16 15		1 - 18 pdr gun with B m demanded on 8/5/17 for C.240 Brigade was received & issued.	B m y
"	" 20		1 - 18 pdr carriage demanded for C.241 Brigade on 12/5/17 was received & issued.	B m y

Anthony D Captain
D.A.D.O.S. 48/Division

Army Form C. 2118

WAR DIARY
of
INTELLIGENCE SUMMARY
(Erase heading not required.)

Conference
War Diary
of
Capt: B.M.J Lorman A.D.
D.A.D.O.S. 48 Division
from 1-6-17 to 30-6-17

WAR DIARY
or
INTELLIGENCE SUMMARY
(Erase heading not required.)

Army Form C. 2118

Place	Date	Hour	Summary of Events and Information	Remarks and references to Appendices
H.30.a.2.4.	June 2nd		1 - 18 pdr gun carriage was demanded for C 241 Brigade to replace one condemned by I.O.M.	B.m.V
"	" 6th		1 - 18 pdr gun carriage for C 241 Brigade was replaced by I.O.M and indent cancelled.	B.m.V
"	" "		1 Lewis gun was demanded for 4th R Berks Regt to replace one destroyed by Shell fire	B.m.V
"	" 8th		1 Lewis Gun demanded on 6/6/17 was received & issued.	B.m.V
"	" 9th		1. 3" Stokes gun was demanded for 143rd T.M. Battery to replace one burst.	B.m.V
"	" 12th		1. 3" Stokes Gun demanded on 9/6/17 was received & issued.	B.m.V
"	" 13th		1 - 18 pdr carriage was demanded for C241 Brigade to replace one destroyed by shell fire.	B.m.V
"	" 21st		2. 18 pdr guns were demanded for B. 241 Brigade to replace 2 condemned for wear. B.m.V was demanded.	B.m.V
"	" 26th		2 Lewis Guns were demanded for 6th Bn R Warwickshire Regt to replace 2 lost in action.	B.m.V
"	" 27th		2 Lewis Guns demanded on 26/6/17 were received & issued	B.m.V

R m Thurso Captain
D.A.D.O.S. 48 Division
30/6/17.

Army Form C. 2118

WAR DIARY
or
INTELLIGENCE SUMMARY
(Erase heading not required.)

Vol 28

Confidential.

War Diary

of

Capt. B. M. Thomson R.A.

D.a.d.o.S., 4.8/Division

From 1-7-17 to 31-7-17

WAR DIARY or INTELLIGENCE SUMMARY

Army Form C. 2118

(Erase heading not required.)

Instructions regarding War Diaries and Intelligence Summaries are contained in F.S. Regs., Part II. and the Staff Manual respectively. Title Pages will be prepared in manuscript.

Place	Date	Hour	Summary of Events and Information	Remarks and references to Appendices
H 30 a. 2. 4.	1/7/17		One Lewis Gun for Bucks Bn demanded on 29/6/17 was received & issued.	B m Y
Adanfer.	4/7/17		The Division arrived from H 30 a 2 4.	B m Y
"	6/7/17		One Vickers Gun was demanded for 144 M.G. Coy to replace one unserviceable	B m Y
"	9/7/17		1 Vickers Gun demanded on 6/7/17 for 144 M.G. Coy was received & issued	B m Y
"	14/7/17		1 3" Stokes Gun was demanded for 145" I.M.B. to replace one destroyed	B m Y
"	20/7/17		Condemned by G.O.M.	B m Y
"	21/7/17		1 3" Stokes Gun demanded on 14/7/17 was received & issued.	B m Y
"			The Division moved to Jamba Buzu.	
Jamba Buzu	25/7/17		1 - 4/5" Hows with Carriage (L) - without B M was demanded for D 241 Bgde to replace one destroyed by Enemy Shellfire	B m Y
"	26/7/17		Attachments for Small Arm Respirators were received & issued.	B m Y
"	26/7/17		1 4.5" How without B M was demanded for D 240 Bgde to replace one condemned by G.O.M. for indentation of bore.	B m Y
"	27/7/17		1 4.5" How with Carriage demanded on 25/7/17 was received & issued	B m Y

1875 W. W593/825 1,000,000 4/15 J.B.C. & A. A.D.S.S./Forms/C. 2118.

Army Form C. 2118

WAR DIARY
or
INTELLIGENCE SUMMARY
(Erase heading not required.)

Place	Date	Hour	Summary of Events and Information	Remarks and references to Appendices
Ganch Res	28/7/17		1 4.5" How" demanded on 26/7/17 was received & issued.	B m Y
"	28/7/17		1 18 pdr Gun Carriage was demanded for D 240 B'gde to replace one totally destroyed	B m Y
			by Shell fire.	
"	29/7/17		1 - 18 pdr gun without T.B.M. was demanded for C. 240 B'gde to replace one destroyed	B m Y
			by Shell fire.	
"	30/7/17		1 - 18 pdr gun demanded on 29/7/17 was received & issued. 5th Army wire G.P. 5"92	B m Y
"	31/7/17		1 - 4.5 How Carriage demanded on 29/7/17 was received & issued. 5th Army wire G.P. 619.	B m Y
"	31/7/17		The Dump was moved from Goneste Breque to A.30.6.5.4 Sheet 2D	B m Y

Bingham
Capt.
R.A.D.O.S. to 5 Divis.

Army Form C. 2118

WAR DIARY
or
INTELLIGENCE SUMMARY
(Erase heading not required.)

Vol 29

Conference
War Diary

Capt. B. M. Thornton R.O. Depp

D.A.D.O.S. 48th Division

From 1-8-17 to 31-8-17

Army Form C. 2118

WAR DIARY
or
INTELLIGENCE SUMMARY

(Erase heading not required.)

Instructions regarding War Diaries and Intelligence Summaries are contained in F. S. Regs., Part II. and the Staff Manual respectively. Title Pages will be prepared in manuscript.

Place	Date	Hour	Summary of Events and Information	Remarks and references to Appendices
Shut'z B A 30 b. s 14	2/8/17		1. .303 Vickers Gun was demanded for 1/5th M G Coy to replace one destroyed by shell fire.	Bm T
"	3/8/17		1. .303 Vickers Gun demanded on 2/8/17 was received & issued.	Bm T
"	2/8/17		1- 18pdr Gun with BM was demanded for 240 Bgde to replace one condemned for scoring.	Bm T
"	3/8/17		1- 18pdr gun demanded on 2/8/17 was received & issued. 5th Army Wire GP 654	Bm T
"	2/8/17		1- 18pdr gun carriage with sights was demanded for 241 Bgde to replace 1 destroyed by shell fire	Bm T
"	8/8/17		1- 18pdr gun carriage demanded on 2/8/17 was received & issued.	Bm T
"	8/8/17		1. Lewis Gun was demanded for 4/12 R. Berks to replace one destroyed by shell fire	Bm T
"	9/8/17		1. Lewis Gun demanded on 8/8/17 was received & issued	Bm T
"	9/8/17		1. Lewis Gun was demanded for Bucks Bn to replace one destroyed by shellfire	Bm T
"	10/8/17		1. Lewis Gun demanded on 9/8/17 was received & issued	Bm T
"	10/8/17		2- Lewis Guns were demanded for 5th Bn Gloucester Regt to replace 2 destroyed by shellfire	Bm T

Army Form C. 2118

WAR DIARY
or
INTELLIGENCE SUMMARY

(Erase heading not required.)

Instructions regarding War Diaries and Intelligence Summaries are contained in F. S. Regs., Part II. and the Staff Manual respectively. Title Pages will be prepared in manuscript.

Place	Date	Hour	Summary of Events and Information	Remarks and references to Appendices
A 30 b 5 u	10/8/17		1 - 18 Pdr gun with B.m was demanded for C 240 Bgde to replace one condemned by 90 A for Scoring	BMT
"	10/8/17		1 - 4.5" Hos Carriage was demanded for D 241 Bgde to replace one destroyed by shell fire	BMT
"	11/8/17		1 - 18 pdr gun demanded on 10/8/17 was received & issued. 5th Army Wis G.P.749	BMT
"	11/8/17		2 - Lewis Guns demanded for 5th Bn Gloucester Regt were received & issued.	BMT
"	11/8/17		1 - .303 Vickers Gun was demanded for 145 m.G.by to replace one destroyed by shell fire.	BMT
"	11/8/17		1 - .303 Vickers Gun were demanded for 143 m.G.by to replace one destroyed by shell fire.	BMT
"	12/8/17		1 - 4.5" Hos Carriage demanded on 10/8/17 was received & issued.	BMT
"	13/8/17		2 - .303 Vickers Guns demanded on 11/8/17 for 143 & 145 m.G.by were received & issued.	BMT

Army Form C. 2118

WAR DIARY
or
INTELLIGENCE SUMMARY
(Erase heading not required.)

Instructions regarding War Diaries and Intelligence Summaries are contained in F. S. Regs., Part II and the Staff Manual respectively. Title Pages will be prepared in manuscript.

Place	Date	Hour	Summary of Events and Information	Remarks and references to Appendices
A.30.b.6.w.	13/8/17		1 - Lewis Gun was demanded for 7th Bn R. Warwickshire Regt to replace one destroyed by shellfire	A.m.T
"	13/8/17		1 - 18 pdr gun without B.M. was demanded for A.241 Bgde to replace one condemned by I.O.M. for scoring.	B.m.T
"	13/8/17		1 - 3" Stokes mortar was demanded for 143 I.M. Battery to replace one destroyed by shellfire.	B.m.T
"	14/8/17		1 - Lewis Gun demanded on 13/8/17 was received & issued	B.m.T
"	14/8/17		1 - 3" Stokes mortar demanded on 13/8/17 was received & issued	B.m.T
"	14/8/17		1 - Lewis Gun was demanded for 7th Bn. R. Warwickshire Regt to replace one destroyed by shellfire.	B.m.T
"	15/8/17		1 - Lewis Gun demanded on 14/8/17 was received & issued. 1 - Vickers gun demanded for 145 M.G. Coy to replace one destroyed by shell fire. 1 - .303 B. were demanded & issued same day.	B.m.T
"	15/8/17		1 - 18 pdr gun without B.M. demanded on 13/8/17 was received & issued. 3rd Army via GPBoS	P.m.T
"	16/8/17		1 - .303 Vickers Gun was demanded for 144 M.G. Coy to replace one destroyed by shellfire.	B.m.T

1875 Wt. W303/826 1,000,000 4/15 J.B.C. & A. A.D.S.S./Forms/C.2118.

Army Form C. 2118

WAR DIARY
or
INTELLIGENCE SUMMARY
(Erase heading not required.)

Instructions regarding War Diaries and Intelligence Summaries are contained in F.S. Regs., Part II. and the Staff Manual respectively. Title Pages will be prepared in manuscript.

Place	Date	Hour	Summary of Events and Information	Remarks and references to Appendices
A.S.O.S.Y.	17/8/17		1 - Lewis Gun was collected from 18th Corps to Regt. Dump & issued to 7th Bn. R. Warwickshire Regt. to replace 1 destroyed by shellfire.	B my
"	17/8/17		1 - .303 Vickers Gun was demanded for 144 M.G. Coy to replace one destroyed by shell fire & issued. received	B my
"	17/8/17		1 - 4.5" Hows, was demanded for D/186 Bde to replace one completely destroyed by shell fire. with carriage	B my
"	18/8/17		2 - .303 Vickers Guns were demanded for 143 M.G. Coy to replace 2 damaged by shell fire beyond local repair. Received & issued same evening.	B my
"	18/8/17		1 - 4.5" Hows with carriage demanded on 17/8/17 was received & issued. 3rd Army Wire G.P. 858.	G my
"	18/8/17		1 - 18 pdr gun with B.M. was demanded for B/186 Bde to replace one condemned by 9 O.M. for scrap.	A my
"	18/8/17		1 - 18 pdr gun demanded on 18/8/17 was received & issued. 3rd Army Wire G.P. 862.	A my
"	19/8/17		15 - .303 Lewis Guns were demanded as follows: 2 for 4th Ox & Bucks Rgt, 1 for 4th R= Glost. Rgt, 3 for 7th R= Worcester Rgt, 2 for 4th R= R. Bucks Rgt to replace those destroyed by shell fire - also 7 for Bucks R= to replace those lost in action.	B my
"	19/8/17		1 - .303 Vickers Gun was demanded for 143 M.G. Coy to replace one damaged by shell fire & beyond local repair.	B my

Army Form C. 2118

WAR DIARY
or
INTELLIGENCE SUMMARY
(Erase heading not required.)

Instructions regarding War Diaries and Intelligence Summaries are contained in F. S. Regs., Part II. and the Staff Manual respectively. Title Pages will be prepared in manuscript.

Place	Date	Hour	Summary of Events and Information	Remarks and references to Appendices
A.30.b.64	19/8/17		3 - 3" Stokes mortars were demanded for 143 T.M. Battery to replace 3 destroyed by shell fire.	B my T
"	19/8/17		1 - 18 pdr gun with 1" B.M. was demanded for T.B.240 Bgde to replace one condemned by G.O.M. for scoring.	B my T
"	20/8/17		1 - 18 pdr gun demanded on 19/8/17 was received & issued. 3rd Army WO G.F.877.	B my T
"	20/8/17		3 - 3" Stokes mortars demanded on 19/8/17 were received & issued.	B my T
"	20/8/17		15 - Lewis Guns demanded on 19/8/17 were received & issued.	B my T
"	20/8/17		2 - Lewis Guns were demanded & received for 1st 6/3rd Staff Regt. to replace 2 destroyed by shell fire.	B my T
"	20/8/17		1 - .303 Vickers Gun was demanded & received for 143 M.G. Coy to replace one destroyed by shell fire.	B my T
"	20/8/17		1 - .303 Vickers Gun demanded on 19/8/17 was received & issued.	B my T
"	21/8/17		1 - .303 Vickers Gun was demanded for 143 M.G. Coy to replace one destroyed by shell fire.	B my T
"	21/8/17		1 - .303 Vickers Gun demanded on 21/8/17 was received & issued.	B my T

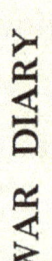

WAR DIARY
or
INTELLIGENCE SUMMARY

(Erase heading not required.)

Army Form C. 2118

Place	Date	Hour	Summary of Events and Information	Remarks and references to Appendices
A30.65¼	22/8/17		1 - 18 pdr gun complete with carriage & limber was demanded for C.241 Bgde to replace complete destroyed by shell fire.	BM &
"	22/8/17		1 - Wagon Ammunition 18pdr was demanded for 48th D.A.C. to replace one condemned by I.O.M. as "beyond local repair" owing to north shell fire.	BM &
"	23/8/17		1 - 18pdr gun & carriage was demanded on 22/8/17 for C.241 Bgde was received & issued 3rd Army via G.P.10.3	BM &
"	23/8/17		1 - Lewis Gun was demanded for 6th Bn. R. Warwickshire Regt. to replace one lost in action.	BM &
"	24/8/17		1 - Lewis Gun demanded on 23/8/17 for 6th Bn. R. Warwickshire Regt. was received & issued	BM &
"	24/8/17		1. Limber 18 pdr carriage demanded on 22/8/17 for C.241 Bgde, was also 1 wagon ammunition 18 pdr demanded on 22/8/17 for D.A.C. was received & issued	BM &
"	24/8/17		1. Limber 18pdr carriage was demanded for B.241 Bgde to replace one condemned by I.O.M. "Beyond local repair".	BM &
"	25/8/17		1 Carriage 18pdr was demanded for C.240 Bgde to replace one condemned by I.O.M. for excessive wear	BM &
"	25/8/17		1 Carriage 4.5 How was demanded for D.240 Bgde to replace one destroyed by shell fire	BM &

WAR DIARY or INTELLIGENCE SUMMARY

Army Form C. 2118

Place	Date	Hour	Summary of Events and Information	Remarks and references to Appendices
A.30.6.5.4	25/8/17		1 limber 18pdr was demanded for C/241 Bgde to replace one condemned by B.O. m. as "Beyond local repair".	A.m.Y
"	25/8/17		2 .303 Vickers Guns were demanded for 143 M.G. Coy to replace 2 destroyed by shell fire.	B.m.Y
"	26/8/17		1- Carriage 18pdr demanded for C/240 Bgde on 25/8/17 was received & issued. 5th Army Wire GP/1022	C.m.Y
"	26/8/17		2- .303 Vickers Guns demanded on 25/8/17 for 143 M.G. Coy were received & issued.	D.m.Y
"	26/8/17		1. Lewis Gun was demanded for 5th Bn Warwickshire Regt to replace one lost in action.	E.m.Y
"	27/8/17		1. Lewis Gun demanded for 5th Bn R. Warwickshire Regt was received & issued	F.m.Y
"	27/8/17		1 limber 18pdr Carriage demanded for 241 Bgde on 24/8/17 was received & issued.	G.m.Y
"	29/8/17		The Dump was moved to Scherts Camp Janita Bugen.	H.m.Y
Janita Bugen	29/8/17		1 limber 4.5 How was demanded for D/241 Bgde to replace one condemned by B.O. as "Beyond local repair"	I.m.Y
"	30/8/17		1 limber 18pdr demanded for C/241 Bgde on 25/8/17 was received & issued.	J.m.Y. K.m.Y
"	31/8/17		1- .303 Vickers Gun was demanded for 145 M.G. Coy to replace one lost in action	L.m.Y
"	31/8/17		1. .303 Vickers Gun demanded on 30/8/17 for 145 M.G. Coy was received & issued.	M.m.Y

Army Form C. 2118

WAR DIARY
or
INTELLIGENCE SUMMARY
(Erase heading not required.)

Place	Date	Hour	Summary of Events and Information	Remarks and references to Appendices
Gondstr Reign	31/8/17		1. Limber 4.5" How demanded on 29/8/17 for D 241 Bgde was received & issued.	Point
" "	31/8/17		5 Lewis Guns were demanded for 5th Bn R Warwickshire Regt, 12 for 6th Bn R War Regt, 5 for 7th Bn R War Regt & 5 for 8th Bn R War Regt also 3 Vickers Guns for 143 M.G. Coy to replace a similar number lost in action & destroyed by shellfire.	Point

Bm Thor LD Captain
A.D.O.S. 48/Division

Army Form C. 2118

WAR DIARY
or
INTELLIGENCE SUMMARY
(Erase heading not required.)

Confidential

War Diary of
Capt. B.M. Johnson A.D.V.S.
D.A.D.V.S. 48th Division
From 1-9-17 to 30-9-17.

Vol 30

Army Form C. 2118

WAR DIARY
or
INTELLIGENCE SUMMARY
(Erase heading not required.)

Instructions regarding War Diaries and Intelligence Summaries are contained in F. S. Regs., Part II. and the Staff Manual respectively. Title Pages will be prepared in manuscript.

Place	Date	Hour	Summary of Events and Information	Remarks and references to Appendices
	1917			
Janets Auger	Sept 1st		1 - 4.5" How Carriage demanded for D 240 Bgde on 25/8/17 was received & issued.	Bm Y
"	" 1st		Jn 27 Lewis Guns & 3 Vickers Guns demanded on 31/8/17 were received & issued.	Bm Y
"	" 1st		1 - 3" Stokes Gun was demanded for 143 T.M. Battery to replace one destroyed by Shell fire	Bm Y
"	" 1st		2 Lewis Guns were demanded for 8th Bn Worcester Regt to replace 2 lost in action.	Bm Y
"	" 2nd		1 - 3" Stokes Gun & 2 Lewis Guns demanded on 1/9/17 was received & issued.	Bm Y
"	" 2nd		1 .303 Lewis Gun was demanded for 5th Bn R. Sussex Regt to replace one destroyed by shell fire.	Bm Y
"	"		2 - .303 Vickers Guns were demanded for 143 M.G. Coy to replace 2 lost in action.	Bm Y
"	" 3rd		1 Lewis Gun & 2 Vickers Guns demanded on 2/9/17 were received & issued.	Bm Y
"	"		1 - .303 Vickers Gun was demanded for 144 M.G. Coy to replace one lost in action	Bm Y
"	" 4th		1 - .303 Vickers Gun demanded on 3/9/17 for 144 M.G. Coy was received & issued.	Bm Y
"	" 5th		1 - 18 pdr Gun & Carriage was demanded for A.241 Bgde to replace ones destroyed	Bm Y
"	"		by shell fire.	
"	" 6th		1 - 18 pdr Gun & Carriage demanded for A.241 Bgde on 5/9/17 was received & issued. 5th Army wire C.Press	Bm Y
"	" 7th		1 - 18 pdr Gun with R.M. was demanded for C.241 Bgde to replace one destroyed	Bm Y
			by shell fire. This was received the same evening.	

WAR DIARY / INTELLIGENCE SUMMARY

Army Form C. 2118

Place	Date	Hour	Summary of Events and Information	Remarks and references to Appendices
Gouzeaucourt	Sept 7th		1 - .303 Vickers Gun was demanded for 143 Bgde M.G Coy to replace one lost in action	B m 7
"	" 8th		1 - .303 Vickers Gun demanded on 7/9/17 was received & issued.	B m 7
"	" 12th		1 - 4.5 Hows with B.m was demanded for D 240 Bgde to replace one destroyed by shell fire.	B m 7
"	" 12th		2. 4.5 How Carriages complete with Sights, were demanded for D 240 Bgde to replace Sights destroyed by shellfire. These were received & issued the same evening.	B m 7
"	" 13th		1 - 4.5 Hows demanded on 12/9/17 for D 240 Bgde was received & issued.	B m 7
"	" 13th		1 - 4.5 How & carriage complete were demanded for D 240 Bgde to replace Sights completely destroyed by Shellfire. These were received & issued same evening.	B m 7
"	"		1 - 4.5 How & carriage complete was demanded for D 240 Bgde to replace Sights destroyed by shell fire	B m 7
"	"		1 - 18 pdr gun with B.m was demanded for C. 240 Bgde to replace one destroyed by Shell fire	B m 7
"	" 14		1 - 4.5 How & Carriage also demanded for D 240 Bgde also 1 - 18 pdr gun for C 240 Bgde on 13/9/17 were received & issued	B m 7
"	" 17th		The Division moved to Zuthpeque	B m 7
Zuthpeque	" 23rd		1 Lewis Gun was demanded for 7th Bn Worcester Regt - to replace one lost in action.	B m 7

Army Form C. 2118

WAR DIARY
INTELLIGENCE SUMMARY
(Erase heading not required.)

Instructions regarding War Diaries and Intelligence Summaries are contained in F. S. Regs., Part II. and the Staff Manual respectively. Title Pages will be prepared in manuscript.

Place	Date	Hour	Summary of Events and Information	Remarks and references to Appendices
Luithargen	27"		1 Lewis gun demanded on 23rd received	S/C.
A27D 50 Sheet 28	28.		Divisund moved from Luithargen to A 27 D 50 Sheet 28.	S/C.
"	29		1 Vickers gun demanded for 1m 5" H.g.C. in place one damaged by shell fire	S/C.
"	30		1 Vickers gun demanded on 29th received	S/C.

S/C. Cannel Capt.
for D.A.D.O.S. 48th Division

Army Form C. 2118.

WAR DIARY
or
INTELLIGENCE SUMMARY.
(Erase heading not required.)

WO 31

Conference
War Diary
of
Capt. R.M.T. Rowan. A.D.
Canst. 48 Division
From 1·10·17 to 31·10·17.

WAR DIARY
or
INTELLIGENCE SUMMARY

(Erase heading not required.)

Army Form C. 2118

Instructions regarding War Diaries and Intelligence Summaries are contained in F. S. Regs., Part II. and the Staff Manual respectively. Title Pages will be prepared in manuscript.

Place	Date	Hour	Summary of Events and Information	Remarks and references to Appendices
A 27.d.60 Shut 28	5/10/17		1 - 303 Vickers Gun was demanded for 145 Bgde to replace one destroyed by Shell fire	B & J
" " "	6/10/17		1. 303 Vickers Gun demanded on 5/10/17 was received & issued	B & J
" " "	6/10/17		3. 303 Vickers Guns were demanded for 143 Bgde & 1 for 144 Bgde to replace others destroyed by Shell fire	B & J
" " "	6/10/17		4. 303 Vickers Guns demanded on 6/10/17 were received & issued	B & J
" " "	7/10/17		The Dump was moved to G.1.6.18.	B & J
G.1.6.18	11/10/17		11 - Lewis Guns were demanded: 7 for 5th R. Warwickshire Regt., 1 for 7th R. War Regt. & 3 for 8th R. War Regt. to replace others destroyed by Shell fire. These were received the same afternoon.	B & J
" "	11/10/17		11 Lewis Guns were demanded for 8th Bn R. War Regt. to replace 10 lost in action & 1 destroyed by shell fire	B & J
" "	12/10/17		11 Lewis Guns demanded on 11/10/17 were received & issued.	B & J
" "	13/10/17		The Division moved to Gouves.	B & J
Gouves	14/10/17		1. 303 Vickers Gun was demanded for 143 M.G. Coy also 1 Lewis Gun for Butler A.T. & 1 Lewis Gun for 4th R. Butes, all to replace others destroyed by shell fire	B & J
" "	15/10/17		5. 303 Vickers Guns were demanded for 144 M.G. Coy to replace others destroyed in action	B & J
" "	16/10/17		1 Lewis Gun was demanded for 7th R. Worcester Regt. to replace one lost in action	B & J
" "	17/10/17		The Division moved to La Fayetti	B & J

Army Form C. 2118.

WAR DIARY
or
INTELLIGENCE SUMMARY.
(Erase heading not required.)

Instructions regarding War Diaries and Intelligence Summaries are contained in F. S. Regs., Part II. and the Staff Manual respectively. Title pages will be prepared in manuscript.

Place	Date	Hour	Summary of Events and Information	Remarks and references to Appendices
La Fargette	17/10/17		7 Lewis Guns were demanded 2 for 6th Gloster Regt & 5 for 8th Worcester Regt to replace others lost in action.	BmT
"	17/10/17		6 Vickers Guns & 3 Lewis Guns demanded on 14/10/17, 16/10/17, 18/10/17 & 17/10/17 were received	BmT
"	18/10/17		2 Lewis Guns were demanded for 4th Bn Gloster Regt to replace others, one lost in action & one unserviceable.	BmT
"	18/10/17		7 Lewis Guns demanded on 17/10/17 were received	BmT
"	18/10/17		2 Lewis Guns were demanded for 7th Bn Worcester Regt to replace 2 lost in action	BmT
"	19/10/17		2 Lewis Guns were demanded on 18/10/17 and 19/10/17 were received	BmT
"	21/10/17		4 Lewis Guns demanded with P.M. & 1 carriage 18pdr were demanded for C 241 Bgde to replace same area	BmT
"	22/10/17		2 - 18pdr guns with P.M. & 1 carriage 18pdr were demanded the Division moving to a new area others left in 15 & 20 Workshops on beyond local repair.	BmT
"	23/10/17		1 - 303 Lewis Gun was demanded for Bucks Bn to replace one beyond local repair.	BmT
"	23/10/17		2 - 18pdr guns & 1 carriage demanded on 22/10/17 were cancelled, the 2 guns & 1 carriage having been re-consigned by 90 & 15 & 20 Workshops	BmT
"	24/10/17		1 - Lewis Gun demanded on 23/10/17 for Bucks Bn was received	BmT
"	24/10/17		2 Lewis Guns were demanded for 8th & 6th Worcester Regt to replace 2 beyond local repair	BmT
"	25/10/17		1 - 18pdr Gun without P.M. was demanded for A.240 Bgde to replace one condemned for excessive wear.	BmT

Army Form C. 2118.

WAR DIARY
or
INTELLIGENCE SUMMARY.
(Erase heading not required.)

Instructions regarding War Diaries and Intelligence Summaries are contained in F. S. Regs., Part II. and the Staff Manual respectively. Title pages will be prepared in manuscript.

Place	Date	Hour	Summary of Events and Information	Remarks and references to Appendices
Alphington	26/10/17		2 Lewis Guns demanded for 8th Bn Worcestershire Regt - on 24/10/17 were received	Bm T
"	"		8. 6" Newton Mortars were received.	Bm T
"	"		6. P.B. num reported from the Base to replace 6 A.O.C. personnel classified "A".	Bm T
"	29/10/17		1 .303 Vickers Gun was demanded for 144th M.G. Coy to replace one lost in action.	Bm T
"	31/10/17		1 .303 Vickers Gun demanded on 29/10/17 was received.	Bm T

Bm Fisher Captain
Q a D O S. 48th Division

A 5834 Wt. W4973/M687 750,000 8/16 D. D. & L. Ltd. Forms/C.2118/13.

www.ingramcontent.com/pod-product-compliance
Lightning Source LLC
Chambersburg PA
CBHW081549160426
43191CB00011B/1882